Betty Crocker's

Cookbook for

BOYS & GIRLS

Golden Press • New York
Western Publishing Company, Inc.
Racine, Wisconsin

Director of Photography: Len Weiss

Third Printing, 1977

Copyright © 1975 by General Mills, Inc., Minneapolis, Minnesota.

Printed in the U.S.A. by Western Publishing Company, Inc.
Published by Golden Press, New York, New York.

Golden and Golden Press® are trademarks of Western Publishing Company, Inc.

Library of Congress Catalog Card Number: 74-23006

Contents

5 Cook's Corner

15 Stuff to Snack On

33 Parties and Presents

53 Fresh-Air Foods

65 A Bunch of Breads

85 Mmm—Main Dishes

109 Super Salads and Vegetables

123 Different Desserts

141 Make a Meal

155 Index

Kitchen Quiz

Can you put these kitchen terms where they belong?

Getting Ingredients Ready

CORE (lettuce, apple)

DRAIN (cooked macaroni)

GREASE (pan)

KNEAD (dough)

LIQUEFY (tomatoes)

MELT (chocolate)

PARE (potato)

PEEL (orange)

ROLL OUT (pastry)

SHRED (cabbage)

SNIP (parsley)

1 _____Spread the bottom and sides of a pan with shortening.

2 _____Change a solid food to a liquid by beating it, usually in the blender.

3 _____Pour off liquid or let it run off through the holes in a sieve or colander.

4 _____Cut off the skin.

5 _____Flatten and spread with a rolling pin.

6 _____Cut into thin pieces, using a knife or the large holes of a grater.

7 _____Cut into very small pieces, using scissors.

8 _____Change a solid food to a liquid by heating it.

9 _____Pull off the skin.

10 _____Curve your fingers and fold dough toward you, then push it away with the heels of your hands, using a quick rocking motion.

11 _____Cut out the stem end or remove the seeds.

Mixing Ingredients

MIX (batter)

BEAT (eggs)

WHIP (cream)

FOLD (whipped cream)

TOSS (salad)

STIR (cookie dough)

1 _____Tumble ingredients lightly with a lifting motion.

2 _____Mix gently, bringing a rubber scraper down through a mixture, across the bottom, up and over the top until blended.

3 _____Mix with a circular or figure-8 motion, using a spoon or fork.

4 _____Combine to distribute ingredients evenly, using an electric mixer, blender or spoon.

5 _____To make smooth with a vigorous over-and-over motion, using a spoon, whip or egg beater.

6 _____Beat rapidly to make light and fluffy, using an electric mixer or egg beater.

(Clue: These are numbered from the gentlest action to the most vigorous.)

Cooking

BAKE (cake)

BOIL (water)

BOIL RAPIDLY (jelly)

BROWN (meat)

FRY (potatoes)

SCALD (milk)

SIMMER (soup)

DOT (casserole)

GARNISH (salad)

COOL (cookies)

REFRIGERATE (pudding)

1 _____Cook in enough fat to cover the bottom of a pan.

2 _____Heat milk until just below the boiling point so a skin forms on top.

3 _____Allow to come down to room temperature.

4 _____Heat until bubbles keep rising and breaking on the surface of a liquid.

5 _____Place in the refrigerator.

6 _____Decorate with pieces of colorful food.

7 _____Cook in the oven.

8 _____Heat until bubbles form rapidly and break on the surface of a liquid.

9 _____Drop bits of butter or cheese here and there over a food.

10 _____Heat liquid until just below the boiling point; bubbles form slowly and collapse *below* the surface.

11 _____Cook on each side until a food changes color, usually in a small amount of fat over medium heat.

Answers

Getting Ingredients Ready
1. Grease; 2. Liquefy; 3. Drain; 4. Pare; 5. Roll out; 6. Shred; 7. Snip; 8. Melt; 9. Peel; 10. Knead; 11. Core.

Mixing Ingredients
1. Toss; 2. Fold; 3. Stir; 4. Mix; 5. Beat; 6. Whip.

Cooking
1. Fry; 2. Scald; 3. Cool; 4. Boil; 5. Refrigerate; 6. Garnish; 7. Bake; 8. Boil rapidly; 9. Dot; 10. Simmer; 11. Brown.

Utensils You Should Have

Apple corer

Long serrated knife

Sharp knife

Custard cups
(6- and 10-ounce)

Mixing bowls (set of 3)

Kitchen scissors

Can opener

Ice-cream scoop

Potato masher

Vegetable parer

Cookie cutter

Biscuit cutter

For Preparation

Vegetable brush

Timer

Egg beater

Pastry brush

Strainer

Cutting board

Covered rolling pin
and board

Colander

Melon baller

Ruler

For Measuring

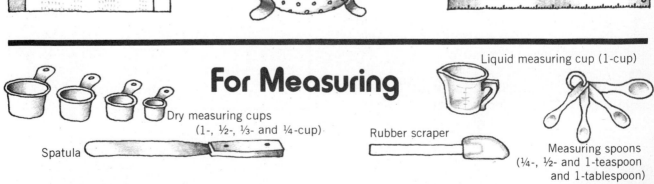

Dry measuring cups
(1-, ½-, ⅓- and ¼-cup)

Liquid measuring cup (1-cup)

Rubber scraper

Measuring spoons
(¼-, ½- and 1-teaspoon
and 1-tablespoon)

Spatula

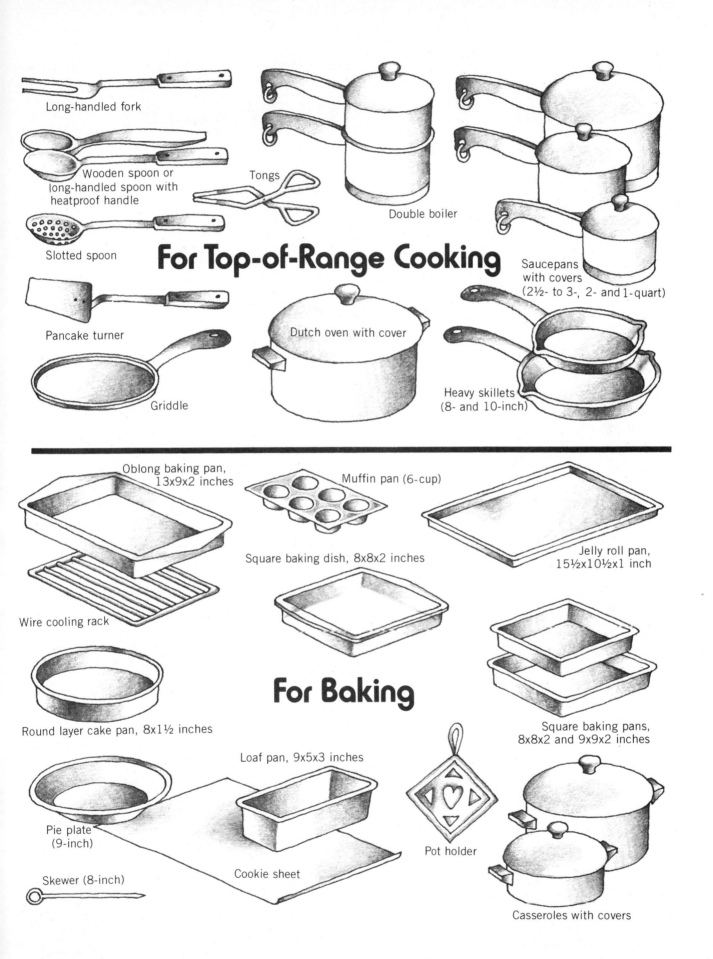

Long-handled fork

Wooden spoon or long-handled spoon with heatproof handle

Slotted spoon

Tongs

Double boiler

For Top-of-Range Cooking

Saucepans with covers (2½- to 3-, 2- and 1-quart)

Pancake turner

Griddle

Dutch oven with cover

Heavy skillets (8- and 10-inch)

Oblong baking pan, 13x9x2 inches

Muffin pan (6-cup)

Jelly roll pan, 15½x10½x1 inch

Square baking dish, 8x8x2 inches

Wire cooling rack

For Baking

Round layer cake pan, 8x1½ inches

Square baking pans, 8x8x2 and 9x9x2 inches

Loaf pan, 9x5x3 inches

Pie plate (9-inch)

Pot holder

Skewer (8-inch)

Cookie sheet

Casseroles with covers

Kitchen Math

3 teaspoons = 1 tablespoon
4 tablespoons = ¼ cup
5 tablespoons plus 1 teaspoon = ⅓ cup
8 tablespoons = ½ cup
16 tablespoons = 1 cup
2 cups = 1 pint
4 cups = 1 quart
2 quarts = ½ gallon

Butter or Margarine

4 sticks (1 pound) = 2 cups
1 stick (¼ pound) = ½ cup
½ stick (⅛ pound) = ¼ cup

Baking dishes are glass; baking pans are metal. Use shiny metal pans to make biscuits, muffins, cakes, cookies and yeast rolls a light brown. Use glass and dull metal pans for pies, breads and hot dishes. Follow the manufacturer's directions for pans with a non-stick coating.

Using Appliances

The Oven

- Arrange the shelves before you turn on the oven.
- Allow plenty of air space around each thing you're baking—no containers should touch.
- Alternate foods on each shelf so that one isn't directly over another.
- Use a tight-fitting cover or aluminum foil when the recipe calls for covering.
- Close the oven door quickly so heat won't be lost.

The Range

- Put large pans on large burners and small pans on small burners. Turn the handles so they don't stick out over the edge of the range, and make sure they're not over another burner either.

The Microwave Oven

- Read the instruction booklet to find out the correct times and kinds of foods your oven can handle.
- Cover most foods to prevent spattering.
- Allow a few minutes' standing time after cooking foods, since they keep on cooking when you take them out of the oven.
- Be careful not to burn yourself. Microwaves go right through containers without heating them, but the food may make them hot.
- See pages 19, 56, 67 and 84 for microwave instructions with recipes.

How to Measure

All-purpose flour: Dip from canister with dry measuring cup. Level with spatula.

Granulated sugar: Measure like flour.

Powdered sugar: Spoon lightly into dry measuring cup. Level with spatula. To remove lumps, press through sieve.

Brown sugar: Pack firmly into dry measuring cup. Level with spatula.

Buttermilk baking mix: Spoon lightly into dry measuring cup over waxed paper. Level with spatula. Baking mix will be lumpy. Pour excess from paper back into box.

Baking powder (and baking soda, cream of tartar, salt, spices): Dip and fill measuring spoon. Level with spatula.

Shredded cheese (and soft crumbs, shredded coconut, raisins, shelled nuts): Pack lightly into dry measuring cup until level.

Soft shortening: Pack firmly into dry measuring cup. Level with spatula and remove with rubber scraper.

Butter or margarine: Unwrap and cut, then soften at room temperature. (Use regular margarine bought in sticks.)

Molasses (and corn syrup): Pour into liquid measuring cup. Remove with rubber scraper.

Vanilla: Pour into measuring spoon held over custard cup or small bowl to catch any overflow.

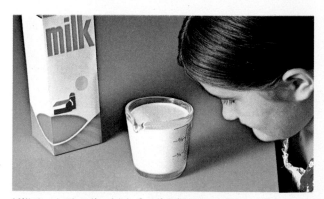

Milk (and other liquids): Set liquid measuring cup on counter, pour in liquid and bend down to check the correct amount at eye level.

Play It Safe!

1 Before you use a sharp knife, can opener, broiler, blender, mixer or microwave oven, be sure someone older is in the kitchen to help you.

2 Ask someone older to drain foods cooked in lots of hot water (like macaroni and spaghetti). If it isn't done just right, the steam could cause a burn.

3 Turn the handles of saucepans on the range away from you so they won't catch on anything and tip over (and be sure they're not over another burner).

4 Dry your hands after you wash them to avoid slippery fingers and shocks from electrical outlets.

5 Wipe up spills right away to avoid slippery floors.

6 Always turn the sharp edge of a knife or vegetable parer away from you and your hand when you chop or pare foods.

7 To avoid burns, use thick, dry pot holders, not thin ones or wet ones.

8 Turn off the blender or mixer before you scrape the side of the container or bowl so the scraper won't get caught in the blades.

9 Turn off the mixer and be sure it's unplugged whenever you put the beaters in or take them out.

10 Never disconnect an appliance by pulling the cord. Pull the plug instead.

Cook's Checklist

☐ Check with the grown-ups in your family for a convenient time to make a recipe.

☐ Wash your hands and wear an apron. Tie back your hair if it's long.

☐ Get out a tray, measuring cups and spoons and a spatula for leveling the ingredients you measure.

☐ Read the recipe all the way through.

☐ Get out all the ingredients and utensils listed in the recipe. Put them on the tray. Then when the tray is empty, you'll know you haven't left out any ingredients.

☐ Clean up as you go along. As you finish using a utensil, put it in warm, soapy water to soak. Oops! Don't put the knives in! When you wash them, be careful of those sharp blades.

☐ Rinse dishes that have had eggs, milk or mashed potatoes in them in cold water first, then in warm water.

☐ Finish washing and drying your utensils and put them away. Wash the counters and leave the kitchen clean and neat.

☐ Check the range to be sure the oven and surface units are turned off and wiped clean.

☐ Cook's reward: delicious results!

Table Talk

A nice-looking table makes mealtime more fun. Correct table setting means:

1 Dinner plate in center, 1 inch from edge of table.

2 Knife to right of plate, blade toward plate.

3 Spoon to right of knife.

4 Fork(s) to left of plate, tines up.

5 Water glass directly above point of knife.

6 Cup and saucer to right of spoon.

7 Salad plate to left of fork(s).

8 Napkin to left of fork(s) with the open corner toward you.

When you're out and in doubt—work from the outside in. Forks and spoons are placed with the piece to be used first on the outside.

But more important than which fork you use and how you hold it is *you*. Wash up before you go to the table . . . sit up straight . . . ask for what you want instead of reaching . . . remember to say "please" and "thank you" . . . take reasonable portions and small bites . . . butter your bread or roll one bite-size portion at a time . . . spoon your soup in the direction of boats sailing away from you . . . ask to be excused when you're finished eating.

Remember that good manners means being thoughtful of others. So wear a smile when you come to the table and try to make mealtime a pleasant time for everyone in your family—that way you'll enjoy it too!

Pictured: Quick-Energy Pickups (page 32), Apple-Cheese Snack (page 16) and Tomato Mush (page 23)

Apple-Cheese Snack

Pictured on page 15.

1 snack.

Utensils	Ingredients
Apple corer	1 red or yellow apple
Cutting board	Small chunk of your
Sharp knife	favorite cheese (Ched-
Small plate	dar, American, Swiss)

1 Wash and core 1 apple. Cut into quarters on cutting board, then cut each quarter into 4 or 5 slices. Arrange in circle on plate.

2 Cut the cheese into wedges and put them in the center of the plate. Munch and crunch!

Chocolate-Banana Yum-Yums

12 yum-yums.

Utensils	Ingredients
Cutting board	3 medium bananas
Table knife	Finely chopped nuts or
12 wooden ice-cream	your favorite dry cereal
sticks	¾ cup milk chocolate
Cookie sheet	chips
Waxed paper	3 tablespoons butter or
Small saucepan	margarine
Long-handled spoon	
Spatula	
Aluminum foil	

1 Peel 3 bananas and cut each crosswise into 4 pieces of equal size on cutting board. Poke an ice-cream stick into each piece and place on ungreased cookie sheet. Freeze about 2 hours or until banana pieces are firm.

2 Spread the finely chopped nuts on waxed paper. Or if you like, crush the cereal with your hands onto the waxed paper.

3 Heat ¾ cup chocolate chips and 3 tablespoons butter in saucepan over low heat until the chocolate chips melt, stirring frequently. Remove from heat.

4 Dip the banana pieces into the chocolate mixture, spreading it over them with spatula. Roll the banana pieces in the nuts or cereal.

5 Cover the cookie sheet with waxed paper.

6 Place the banana pieces on the waxed paper and freeze until coating is firm. When firm, wrap each in aluminum foil and return to the freezer. Remove from the freezer 15 minutes before serving.

VARIATION

Pink or Yellow Banana Yum-Yums: Follow recipe for Chocolate-Banana Yum-Yums except—omit the chocolate chips. Heat the 3 tablespoons butter or margarine and 3 tablespoons milk in saucepan over low heat until the butter melts, stirring frequently. Stir in 1 package (14.3 ounces) creamy cherry or lemon frosting mix. Continue cooking until the frosting is liquid, stirring frequently. Continue as directed except—after wrapping, refrigerate until serving time. Do not return to the freezer.

Banana Boats

4 boats.

Utensils	Ingredients
Cutting board	¼ cup salted peanuts
Sharp knife	4 large bananas
Kitchen scissors	1 carton (4½ ounces)
Small bowl	frozen whipped
Teaspoon	topping, thawed
Rubber scraper	4 maraschino cherries

1 Chop ¼ cup peanuts on cutting board.

2 Gently wash 4 bananas. Carefully slit top of each banana peel lengthwise, leaving about 1 inch uncut at each end. Cut away about ½ inch of the peel on each side of the slit with scissors.

3 Empty the whipped topping into bowl. Scoop out each banana in small pieces with teaspoon into the bowl. Save the banana peel shells. Fold the banana pieces into the topping with rubber scraper.

4 Fill each banana peel shell with ¼ of the banana-topping mixture. Sprinkle with ¼ of the chopped peanuts and top with 1 maraschino cherry.

5 Serve Banana Boats right away or refrigerate as long as 1 hour.

Slit the banana peel, then cut away about ½ inch of the peel on each side of the slit with scissors.

Scoop out small chunks of banana with a teaspoon. Save the banana peel shells to fill later.

Fold the banana pieces into the whipped topping, then fill the shells with the mixture.

Sprinkle each boat with chopped peanuts and top with a maraschino cherry.

Hawaiian Pops

12 pops.

Utensils	Ingredients
1 or 2 muffin pans	1 can (16 ounces) peach
12 paper baking cups	slices
Spoon	About 3 cups red fruit
12 wooden ice-cream	punch drink
sticks or plastic	
spoons	
Table knife	

1 Line 12 muffin cups with baking cups. Divide the peach slices and syrup among the paper-lined cups.

2 Freeze 1 hour or until firm enough to hold an ice-cream stick upright. Poke a stick into each pop.

3 Fill each cup to the top with fruit punch drink (about ¼ cup for each).

4 Freeze about 2 hours or until firm. To loosen, quickly dip each muffin pan almost to the rim in hot water. Loosen the pops with table knife.

5 To serve, peel off the baking cups. (It's a good idea to slide a clean baking cup over each stick to catch drips.)

VARIATION

Pudding Pops: Follow recipe for Hawaiian Pops except—use only 6 muffin cups. In place of the peach slices and syrup, use 1 can (17.5 ounces) chocolate pudding. Place a banana slice in each muffin cup. Fill each cup to the top with pudding. Poke a stick into each pop and continue as directed.

Purple Cow Shakes

3 or 4 shakes.

Utensils	Ingredients
Blender	1 can (6 ounces) frozen
Ice-cream scoop or	grape juice
large spoon	concentrate
	1 cup milk
	2 cups vanilla ice cream

1 Pour the juice concentrate and 1 cup milk into blender container.

2 Scoop in 2 cups ice cream.

3 Cover and blend on high speed 30 seconds. Serve right away.

Note: No blender? Scoop the ice cream into a 2-quart jar with remaining ingredients. Cover tightly and shake. Or beat in a large bowl with an egg beater.

You need at least 3 glasses of milk a day to keep your bones and teeth healthy. Another way to get those good-for-you nutrients is to have 2 slices of cheese or 1 cup of cocoa or 1 malt instead of 1 glass of milk.

Here's a milk shake for breakfast time or anytime: Pour 1 cup milk into the blender container. Add 1 envelope (about 1.2 ounces) strawberry- or vanilla- or chocolate-flavored instant breakfast drink mix. Add ¼ cup canned crushed pineapple or 6 canned apricot halves or 1 small banana, peeled and sliced. Cover the container and blend on high speed 5 to 10 seconds or until smooth. Serve right away.

Banana-Orange Junior

3 drinks.

Utensils	Ingredients
Blender	½ cup milk
Ice-cream scoop or	½ cup orange juice
large spoon	2 cups orange sherbet
3 tall glasses	1 banana

1 Pour ½ cup milk and ½ cup orange juice into blender container. Scoop in 1 cup of the sherbet. Peel 1 banana and break it into pieces into the container.

2 Cover and blend on high speed 10 seconds. Pour into 3 glasses. Top each with a scoop of sherbet from the remaining 1 cup. Serve right away.

Rainbow Float

1 float.

Utensils	Ingredients
Tall glass	Red fruit punch drink or
Ice-cream scoop or	fruit juice
large spoon	⅔ cup lemon sherbet
	Chilled carbonated
	lemon-lime soda pop
	or club soda

1 Fill glass halfway to the top with fruit punch drink. Scoop in ⅔ cup sherbet.

2 Fill the glass with soda pop. Serve the float right away.

Cocoa

9 servings.

Utensils	Ingredients
Large saucepan	⅓ cup sugar
Long-handled spoon	⅓ cup cocoa
Egg beater (if you like)	¼ teaspoon salt
	1½ cups water
	4½ cups milk
	¼ teaspoon vanilla

1 Mix ⅓ cup sugar, ⅓ cup cocoa and ¼ teaspoon salt in saucepan. Add 1½ cups water. Heat to boiling, stirring constantly. Boil and stir 2 minutes.

2 Stir in 4½ cups milk. Heat through but do not boil. Add ¼ teaspoon vanilla.

3 Just before serving, beat until foamy or stir until smooth.

Note: The quickest way to make cocoa is with a microwave oven if you have one. Pour chocolate milk to within ½ inch of the top of a mug or cup. Cook uncovered (1 cup at a time) in microwave oven 1 minute 30 seconds or until hot. Place a marshmallow on top of the cocoa and sprinkle with a little cinnamon. Cook 20 seconds longer (if you heat more than 1 cup of cocoa, the cooking time will be longer).

Strawberry Soda

1 soda.

Utensils	Ingredients

Tall glass
Long-handled spoon
Ice-cream scoop or
    large spoon
	2 tablespoons straw-
	    berry ice-cream
	    topping
	2 tablespoons pineapple
	    ice-cream topping
	1½ cups vanilla ice
	    cream
	Chilled carbonated
	    strawberry soda pop

1 Mix 2 tablespoons strawberry topping, 2 tablespoons pineapple topping and ¼ cup of the ice cream in glass.

2 Stir in ¼ cup of the soda pop. Scoop in remaining 1¼ cups ice cream. Fill the glass with soda pop. Serve right away.

Snowcap Eggnog

2 eggnogs.

Utensils	Ingredients
Small bowl Egg beater 2 glasses Spoon	2 eggs 1 cup milk ¼ cup sugar ½ teaspoon vanilla 2 tablespoons vanilla ice cream

1 Beat 2 eggs, 1 cup milk, ¼ cup sugar and ½ teaspoon vanilla in bowl.

2 Pour the eggnog into 2 glasses and top each with a spoonful of ice cream. Serve right away.

Munchy Crunchy Granola

4 cups granola.

Utensils	Ingredients

Kitchen scissors
Jelly roll pan,
    15½ × 10½ × 1 inch,
    or 2 oblong baking
    pans, 13 × 9 × 2
    inches
Spoon
	½ cup dried apples,
	    apricots or mixed fruit
	1½ cups oats
	1 cup golden raisins
	1 package (4 ounces)
	    toasted sunflower nuts
	¼ cup sesame seeds
	¼ cup brown sugar
	    (packed)
	¼ cup salad oil
	2 tablespoons vanilla
	¼ teaspoon salt

1 Heat oven to 350°.

2 Cut ½ cup dried apples into small pieces with scissors.

3 Spread the apple pieces and remaining ingredients in ungreased jelly roll pan. Mix well.

4 Bake in 350° oven 10 minutes. Remove from the oven and stir.

5 Return to the oven and bake 10 minutes more. Use the granola as a topping for cereal or ice cream, or serve in bowls for nibbles, or pack in small plastic bags for snacks or lunch box treats. Store any leftover granola tightly covered in refrigerator.

Snickersnack

About 7 cups snack.

Utensils	Ingredients
Large bowl	4 cups O-shaped puffed
Spoon	oat cereal
Small saucepan	1 can (6½ ounces)
Fork	salted peanuts
	1 cup golden raisins
	¼ cup butter or
	margarine (½ stick)
	1 package (6 ounces)
	semisweet chocolate
	chips

1 Mix 4 cups cereal, the peanuts and 1 cup raisins in bowl.

2 Melt ¼ cup butter in saucepan over low heat.

3 Pour the melted butter over the cereal mixture, using fork to toss lightly until mixture is coated. Sprinkle the chocolate chips over the mixture and toss again. Serve in bowls for nibbles or pack in small plastic bags for snacks or lunch box treats.

Cereal Sundae

1 sundae.

Utensils	Ingredients
Cereal bowl	Your favorite dry cereal
Ice-cream scoop or	Your favorite ice cream
large spoon	

Fill bowl halfway to the top with cereal. Place a large scoop of ice cream in the center. Sprinkle with a little more cereal. Serve right away.

Jeweled Sundaes

8 sundaes.

Utensils	Ingredients
Strainer	1 can (8¾ ounces) fruit
Medium bowl	cocktail
Small bowl	1 package (3 ounces)
Small mixer bowl	cherry-flavored gelatin
Small saucepan	½ cup water
Long-handled spoon	½ cup chilled whipping
Egg beater	cream
Ice-cream scoop or	4 cups vanilla ice cream
large spoon	
8 dessert dishes	
Tablespoon	

1 Empty the fruit cocktail into strainer over medium bowl.

2 Empty the gelatin into small bowl. Take out 1 tablespoon of the gelatin and empty it into small mixer bowl (you will use it to sweeten the whipping cream). Refrigerate bowl.

3 Heat ½ cup water just to boiling in saucepan over medium-high heat. Pour the boiling water over the gelatin in the first bowl. Stir until the gelatin dissolves. Stir in the drained fruit.

4 Pour ½ cup whipping cream into the chilled mixer bowl with the 1 tablespoon gelatin. Beat until stiff.

5 Scoop 4 cups ice cream into 8 dessert dishes (½ cup in each dish). Spoon a few tablespoons of the warm gelatin mixture over the ice cream in each dish and watch it thicken! Spoon 1 or 2 tablespoons of the whipped cream on top of each sundae. Serve right away.

Sundae Steamboats

6 steamboats.

Utensils	Ingredients
Cookie sheet	4 cups corn puff cereal
Large bowl	(chocolate or plain)
18 wooden picks	18 maraschino cherries
Large saucepan	36 miniature marsh-
Long-handled spoon	mallows
6 dessert plates	20 large marshmallows
Ice-cream scoop	2 tablespoons butter or
or large spoon	margarine
	⅛ teaspoon salt
	3 cups strawberry
	ice cream

1 Grease cookie sheet with some butter or margarine.

2 Empty 4 cups cereal into bowl. Poke each wooden pick through 1 maraschino cherry and 1 miniature marshmallow. (You'll poke 3 of these into each steamboat later.)

3 Heat 20 large marshmallows, 2 tablespoons butter and ⅛ teaspoon salt in saucepan over medium heat until marshmallows melt. Stir until smooth. Remove from heat.

4 Pour the marshmallow mixture over the cereal and stir until cereal is coated.

5 Rub some butter on your hands and divide the cereal mixture into 6 parts on the greased cookie sheet. Shape each part into a boat about 6 inches long and 2½ inches wide.

6 Place each boat on a dessert plate and fill with 3 small scoops (about ½ cup) of the ice cream. Poke 1 prepared wooden pick into each scoop of ice cream. Serve right away.

Tomato Mush

Pictured on page 15.

3 drinks.

Utensils	Ingredients
Vegetable parer	1 small carrot
Sharp knife	½ celery stalk
Cutting board	¼ teaspoon salt
Blender	1 teaspoon paprika
	3 ice cubes
	⅔ cup tomato juice

1 Wash and pare 1 carrot. Wash ½ celery stalk and pinch off leaves.

2 Cut the carrot into 1-inch slices and the celery into 1-inch pieces on cutting board. Place in blender container.

3 Add ¼ teaspoon salt, 1 teaspoon paprika, 3 ice cubes and ⅔ cup tomato juice. Cover and blend on high speed 20 seconds. Serve right away.

Vegetable Bugs

Pictured on the back cover.

1 Wash 3 or 4 cherry tomatoes, then attach them in a line with wooden picks. Use 2 whole cloves to make eyes on 1 of the 2 end tomatoes, then make 2 little holes over the cloves and poke in celery leaves. There! You have a flirty caterpillar. (To eat it, take out the wooden picks and cloves.)

2 Wash a small radish and a big red round one. Pare the small radish and attach it to the big one with a wooden pick. Use whole cloves for spots, legs and eyes. Does it look like a ladybug? (To eat it, take out the wooden pick and cloves.)

Raw Vegetable Snacks

Prepare any of the snacks below, then keep them fresh and crisp in a bowl of ice water in the refrigerator. Nibble anytime!

Carrot Curls: Wash and pare some carrots. Make long paper-thin curls by slicing the length of each carrot with a vegetable parer. (Always cut away from your hand!) Roll each slice around your finger, then poke a wooden pick through the carrot curl. Place in ice water in the refrigerator about 1 hour so the curls will hold their shape, then remove the wooden picks.

Celery Curls: Wash some celery stalks and pinch off the leaves. Cut several stalks at a time into 2- or 3-inch lengths on a cutting board. Cut the ends of each length into narrow strips (like fringe). Place in ice water in the refrigerator about 1 hour so the ends will curl.

Radish Fans: Wash and trim some radishes. Make thin parallel cuts in one side of each radish to about ¼ inch from the other side. Place in ice water in the refrigerator about 1 hour so the cuts will open to make a pretty fan.

Zucchini Sticks: Wash a zucchini and cut into short narrow sticks.

Cucumber Sticks: Wash and pare a cucumber and cut into short narrow sticks.

Cauliflowerets: Wash a head of cauliflower under running cold water, then break or cut into bite-size pieces.

Broccoli Buds: Wash some broccoli, then break or cut the buds into bite-size pieces.

Sprinkle Cookies

About 72 cookies.

Utensils	Ingredients
Paper towels	1 can (8½ ounces) fruit
Jelly roll pan,	cocktail
15½ × 10½ × 1 inch	½ cup butter or mar-
Table knife	garine (1 stick)
Wire cooling rack	1 package (19.5 ounces)
Aluminum foil	spice 'n apple cake
	mix with raisins
	3 cups miniature marsh-
	mallows
	2½ cups granola or oats
	1 can (14 ounces)
	sweetened condensed
	milk

1 Heat oven to 350°.

2 Drain the can of fruit cocktail and spread the fruit on paper towels to dry.

3 Heat ½ cup butter in jelly roll pan in 350° oven 2 to 3 minutes or until it melts. Carefully remove the pan from the oven and tilt and turn it until the melted butter covers the bottom completely.

4 Sprinkle the cake mix (dry) evenly over the melted butter. Sprinkle 3 cups miniature marshmallows over the cake mix. Then sprinkle the drained fruit over the marshmallows. Sprinkle 2½ cups granola over the fruit.

5 Pour the condensed milk evenly over the ingredients in the pan.

6 Bake in 350° oven 25 to 30 minutes or until golden brown. Do not overbake! While warm, run knife around the edges of the pan to loosen the sides. Cool on rack. Cut into 1½-inch squares. Wrap any remaining squares in aluminum foil and store at room temperature or freeze as long as 2 months.

Note: In place of the fruit cocktail, you can use 1 cup mixed dried fruit (about 6 ounces), cut up. The cookies will be chewier and drier.

Gingersnaps

About 66 cookies.

Utensils	Ingredients
Small mixer bowl	1 package (14.5 ounces)
Electric mixer	gingerbread mix
Rubber scraper	½ cup milk
Teaspoon	⅓ cup salad oil
Cookie sheet	Sugar (if you like)
Pancake turner	
Wire cooling rack	

1 Heat oven to 375°.

2 Beat all ingredients except sugar in bowl on low speed 30 seconds. Turn off the mixer and scrape the side of the bowl. Beat on medium speed 30 seconds.

3 Drop the dough by rounded teaspoonfuls about 3 inches apart onto ungreased cookie sheet. Sprinkle the tops with sugar.

4 Bake in 375° oven 8 to 10 minutes or until almost no imprint remains when a cookie is touched lightly. Immediately lift the cookies to rack with pancake turner.

Marshmallow Puffs

36 puffs.

Utensils	Ingredients
Kitchen scissors	18 large marshmallows
Glass	36 vanilla or chocolate
Cookie sheet	wafers (about 1½
Small saucepan	inches across)
Long-handled spoon	¾ cup semisweet
	chocolate chips
	3 tablespoons butter or
	margarine

1 Heat oven to 350°.

2 Cut 18 large marshmallows in half with scissors. (Dip the scissors into glass of water to keep the marshmallows from sticking.)

3 Arrange 36 vanilla wafers on ungreased cookie sheet. Place 1 marshmallow half cut side down on each wafer.

4 Bake in 350° oven 4 to 5 minutes or until the marshmallows puff but before they begin to tip over.

5 Refrigerate the cookies on the cookie sheet 10 minutes.

6 While the cookies are cooling, heat ¾ cup chocolate chips and 3 tablespoons butter in saucepan over low heat until chocolate melts, stirring frequently. Remove from heat.

7 Dip the tops of the cooled cookies into the chocolate mixture. Refrigerate about 15 minutes or until set. Store leftover cookies in the refrigerator.

Note: These cookies slide around on the cookie sheet, so be careful!

Big Fat Cookies

Pictured on page 133.

About 30 cookies.

Utensils	Ingredients
Cookie sheet	1 package (18.5 ounces)
Large mixer bowl	yellow or devils food
Electric mixer	cake mix
Rubber scraper	½ cup water
Tablespoon	2 eggs
Pancake turner	1 cup semisweet
Wire cooling rack	chocolate chips

1 Heat oven to 375°. Grease cookie sheet with shortening.

2 Prepare the cake mix as directed on package except—reduce the water to ½ cup. Drop the dough by rounded tablespoonfuls 3 inches apart onto the greased cookie sheet. Sprinkle with 1 cup chocolate chips.

3 Bake in 375° oven 6 to 8 minutes or until almost no impression remains when a cookie is touched lightly. Cool on cookie sheet 1 minute, then lift the cookies to rack with pancake turner.

VARIATION

Gumdrop Cookies: Follow recipe for Big Fat Cookies except—in place of the chocolate chips, use 1 cup small gumdrops. Cut the gumdrops in half so they won't sink to the bottom and stick.

Chocolate Chip Cookies

About 24 cookies.

Utensils	Ingredients
Cookie sheet	¼ cup butter or margarine, softened (½ stick)
Large bowl	
Long-handled spoon	
Teaspoon	⅔ cup brown sugar (packed)
Pancake turner	
Wire cooling rack	1 egg
	1⅓ cups biscuit baking mix
	¼ cup all-purpose flour
	1 package (6 ounces) semisweet chocolate chips

1 Heat oven to 375°. Grease cookie sheet with shortening.

2 Mix ¼ cup butter, ⅔ cup brown sugar and 1 egg in bowl. Stir in 1⅓ cups baking mix and ¼ cup flour and mix until smooth. Stir in the chocolate chips.

3 Drop the dough by rounded teaspoonfuls about 2 inches apart onto the greased cookie sheet.

4 Bake in 375° oven 8 to 10 minutes or until almost no impression remains when a cookie is touched lightly. Immediately lift the cookies to wire cooling rack with pancake turner.

VARIATION

Yo-Yo Cookies: Bake Chocolate Chip Cookies. When cool, put the flat sides of the baked cookies together in pairs, attaching them with your favorite frosting. Tuck the end of a 3-inch licorice string between each pair of cookies if you like.

Favorite Brownies

36 brownies.

Utensils	Ingredients
Oblong baking pan, 13 × 9 × 2 inches	4 ounces unsweetened chocolate
Pastry brush	⅔ cup shortening
Large saucepan	2 cups granulated sugar
Long-handled spoon	4 eggs
Rubber scraper	1 teaspoon vanilla
Wire cooling rack	1¼ cups all-purpose flour*
Table knife	
	1 teaspoon baking powder
	1 teaspoon salt
	1 cup chopped nuts
	Powdered sugar

1 Heat oven to 350°. Generously grease baking pan with shortening, using pastry brush.

2 Heat 4 ounces chocolate and ⅔ cup shortening in saucepan over low heat until the chocolate melts. Remove from heat. Mix in 2 cups granulated sugar, 4 eggs and 1 teaspoon vanilla. Stir in 1¼ cups flour, 1 teaspoon baking powder, 1 teaspoon salt and 1 cup chopped nuts. Spread the batter in the greased pan with rubber scraper.

3 Bake in 350° oven 30 minutes or until the brownies start to pull away from the sides of the pan. Do not overbake!

4 Cool the brownies slightly on rack. Cut into bars, about 2 inches long and 1½ inches wide. Cool completely. Sprinkle with powdered sugar.

* If using self-rising flour, omit the baking powder and salt.

Root Beer Cookies

About 42 cookies.

Utensils	Ingredients
Large bowl	1 cup brown sugar (packed)
Long-handled spoon	½ cup butter or margarine, softened (1 stick)
Cookie sheet	
Teaspoon	
Pancake turner	1 egg
Wire cooling rack	¼ cup buttermilk or water
Waxed paper	
Spoon	1 teaspoon root beer extract
	1¾ cups all-purpose flour*
	½ teaspoon baking soda
	½ teaspoon salt
	Root Beer Glaze (right)

1 Mix 1 cup brown sugar, ½ cup butter and 1 egg in bowl until fluffy. Stir in ¼ cup buttermilk, 1 teaspoon root beer extract, 1¾ cups flour, ½ teaspoon baking soda and ½ teaspoon salt and mix until smooth. Cover and refrigerate at least 1 hour.

2 When the dough has been refrigerated at least 1 hour, heat oven to 400°.

3 Grease cookie sheet with shortening.

4 Drop the dough by rounded teaspoonfuls about 2 inches apart onto the greased cookie sheet.

5 Bake in 400° oven 6 to 8 minutes or until almost no impression remains when a cookie is touched lightly. Immediately lift the cookies to rack with pancake turner.

6 Prepare Root Beer Glaze.

7 Place waxed paper under the rack. Spoon the glaze over the cookies. The glaze that drips onto the waxed paper can be scraped off and used.

* If using self-rising flour, omit the baking soda and salt.

Note: Cookie sheets should always be at least 2 inches narrower all around than your oven to allow air to move around them.

Root Beer Glaze

Utensils	Ingredients
Small bowl	2 cups powdered sugar
Spoon	⅓ cup butter or margarine, softened
	1½ teaspoons root beer extract
	2 tablespoons hot water

Mix in bowl 2 cups powdered sugar and ⅓ cup butter. Stir in 1½ teaspoons root beer extract and 2 tablespoons hot water. Now go back to Step 7.

VARIATION

Brown Sugar Drops: Follow recipe for Root Beer Cookies except—in place of the root beer extract in the cookie and glaze recipes, use vanilla.

Ice-Cream Cookies

About 48 cookies.

Utensils	Ingredients
Ice-cream scoop or large spoon	2 cups chocolate ice cream
Medium bowl	2¼ cups biscuit baking mix
Cookie sheet	¼ cup sugar
Spoon or fork	½ teaspoon cinnamon
Teaspoon	1 package (6 ounces) semisweet chocolate chips
Pancake turner	
Wire cooling rack	

1 Heat oven to 375°.

2 Scoop 2 cups ice cream into bowl. Let stand at room temperature about 5 minutes.

3 Grease cookie sheet with shortening.

4 Stir into the ice cream 2¼ cups baking mix, ¼ cup sugar and ½ teaspoon cinnamon and mix until smooth. Stir in the chocolate chips.

5 Drop the dough by rounded teaspoonfuls about 3 inches apart onto the greased cookie sheet. (Store remaining dough in refrigerator while the cookies are baking.)

6 Bake in 375° oven 8 to 10 minutes or until the tops of the cookies are dry. Cool on the cookie sheet 1 minute, then lift the cookies to rack with pancake turner.

7 Repeat steps 5 and 6 until all the dough is used.

Note: If possible, bake 2 sheets of cookies at a time. For more even heating, try not to put one sheet exactly under the other one in the oven.

Pick-Your-Flavor Cookies

About 36 cookies.

Utensils	Ingredients
Cookie sheet	1 can (16½ ounces) your favorite flavor frosting
Medium bowl	
Long-handled spoon	2 cups biscuit baking mix
Teaspoon	1 egg
Pancake turner	
Wire cooling rack	
Spatula	

1 Heat oven to 375°. Grease cookie sheet with shortening.

2 Measure ¾ cup frosting. (You'll use the remainder later to frost the cookies.)

3 Mix 2 cups baking mix, 1 egg and the ¾ cup frosting in bowl. (The dough will be stiff.)

4 Drop the dough by teaspoonfuls about 2 inches apart onto the greased cookie sheet.

5 Bake 10 to 12 minutes or until almost no impression remains when a cookie is touched lightly. Immediately lift the cookies to rack with pancake turner.

6 When the cookies are cool, spread with remaining frosting, using spatula.

Spicy Date Softies

About 42 softies.

Utensils	Ingredients
Cookie sheet	1 package (14 ounces)
Large bowl	date bar mix
Long-handled spoon	¼ cup hot water
Teaspoon	1 egg
Pancake turner	1 cup raisins
Wire cooling rack	½ cup chopped nuts
	½ teaspoon cinnamon

1 Heat oven to 400°. Grease cookie sheet with shortening.

2 Mix Date Filling from the date bar mix and ¼ cup hot water in bowl. Add Crumbly Mix from the date bar mix and 1 egg and mix thoroughly. Stir in 1 cup raisins, ½ cup chopped nuts and ½ teaspoon cinnamon.

3 Drop the dough by rounded teaspoonfuls about 2 inches apart onto the greased cookie sheet.

4 Bake in 400° oven 8 to 10 minutes or until almost no impression remains when a cookie is touched lightly. Immediately lift the cookies to rack with pancake turner.

VARIATIONS

Apple-Date Softies: Follow recipe for Spicy Date Softies except—in place of the raisins, use 1 cup finely chopped unpared apple.

Pineapple-Date Softies: Follow recipe for Spicy Date Softies except—in place of the hot water, use 1 can (8¼ ounces) crushed pineapple (with syrup). Omit the raisins and cinnamon.

Brownie Slowpokes

66 to 72 slowpokes.

Utensils	Ingredients
Cookie sheet	1 package (22.5 ounces)
Large bowl	fudge brownie mix
Long-handled spoon	⅓ cup water
Teaspoon	2 eggs
Pancake turner	About ½ cup walnut or
Wire cooling rack	pecan halves
Small bowl	1 package (15.4 ounces)
Fork	creamy white or
Spatula	chocolate fudge
	frosting mix
	Hot water

1 Heat oven to 350°.

2 Mix the brownie mix, ⅓ cup water and 2 eggs in large bowl. (The dough will be stiff.)

3 For each cookie, place 3 walnut halves so that they form the letter Y on ungreased cookie sheet. (The cookies should be 2 inches apart.) Drop the dough by rounded teaspoonfuls onto center of each group of nuts.

4 Bake in 350° oven 10 minutes. Cool on the cookie sheet about 2 minutes. Lift the cookies to rack with pancake turner.

5 Prepare the frosting mix as directed on package. Spread a little frosting on each slowpoke with spatula.

Teddy Bear Paws

16 paws.

Utensils	Ingredients
Medium bowl	½ cup granulated sugar
Egg beater	¼ cup butter or mar-
Long-handled spoon	garine, softened
Breadboard and	(½ stick)
pastry cloth	2 tablespoons shortening
Rolling pin and	1 egg
stockinet cover	1 teaspoon vanilla
Custard cup	1¼ cups all-purpose
Cookie sheet	flour*
Table knife	½ teaspoon baking
Spatula	powder
Pancake turner	½ teaspoon salt
Wire cooling rack	About 3 tablespoons
	raspberry jam
	About 3 tablespoons
	chopped nuts
	About 3 tablespoons
	powdered sugar

1 Beat ½ cup granulated sugar, ¼ cup butter, 2 tablespoons shortening, 1 egg and 1 teaspoon vanilla in bowl. Stir in 1¼ cups flour, ½ teaspoon baking powder and ½ teaspoon salt and mix until smooth. Cover and refrigerate at least 1 hour.

2 Cover breadboard with pastry cloth, tucking ends underneath. Cover rolling pin with stockinet cover. For convenience, place some flour in custard cup. Sprinkle the covered board and rolling pin lightly with the flour and rub it in until it disappears.

3 Grease cookie sheet with shortening.

4 When the dough has been refrigerated at least 1 hour, heat oven to 400°.

5 Roll the dough into a 12-inch square on the covered board. Cut into 3-inch squares.

6 Spread about ½ teaspoon jam down the center of each square. Sprinkle the jam on each square with about ½ teaspoon nuts.

7 Fold one edge of the dough over the jam and nuts, then fold the other edge over the top. Lift the unbaked cookies onto the greased cookie sheet with pancake turner.

8 Make 4 or 5 cuts in one long side of each cookie and spread the cuts slightly apart. Sprinkle each cookie with about ½ teaspoon powdered sugar.

9 Bake in 400° oven 6 minutes or until light brown. Lift to rack with pancake turner.

* Do not use self-rising flour in this recipe.

VARIATIONS

Pinwheels: Follow recipe for Teddy Bear Paws except—cut unfolded 3-inch squares diagonally from each corner almost to the center. Fold every other point to the center to make pinwheel. Spoon ½ teaspoon jam onto the center of each pinwheel and sprinkle with ½ teaspoon chopped nuts and ½ teaspoon powdered sugar. Bake as directed.

Lollipops: Follow recipe for Teddy Bear Paws except—do not roll the dough. Drop by teaspoonfuls onto ungreased cookie sheet. Flatten slightly with your fingers. Place 1 wooden ice-cream stick and 1 milk chocolate star on each circle. Top with another teaspoonful of dough and press the dough together with your fingers. Bake as directed about 8 minutes or until light brown.

Mexican Cookies: Follow recipe for Teddy Bear Paws except—in place of the vanilla, use 1 teaspoon anise extract. Cut the 12-inch square into 3-inch flower shapes with a cookie cutter. Sprinkle with colored sugar. Bake as directed.

Roll the cookie dough into a 12-inch square, then cut into 3-inch squares.

Spread jam down the center of each square, then sprinkle the jam with chopped nuts.

Fold one edge over, then fold the other edge over that. (The dough may crack a little bit.)

Make 4 or 5 cuts in one long side of each cookie and spread the cuts slightly apart.

Lollipops, Pinwheels, Teddy Bear Paws and Mexican Cookies

Quick-Energy Pickups

Pictured on page 15.

30 pickups.

Utensils	Ingredients
Waxed paper	3 or 4 square graham
Medium bowl	crackers
Spoon	1 cup powdered sugar
Teaspoon	1 cup crunchy peanut
Cookie sheet	butter
	1 cup semisweet
	chocolate chips
	½ cup instant nonfat
	dry milk
	3 tablespoons water

1 Crush 3 or 4 graham crackers with your fingers onto sheet of waxed paper.

2 Mix remaining ingredients thoroughly in bowl.

3 Shape teaspoonfuls of the mixture into 1-inch balls. Roll the balls in the graham cracker crumbs until coated.

4 Arrange the coated balls on ungreased cookie sheet and refrigerate about 20 minutes or until firm.

Note: In place of the graham crackers, you can use ½ cup prepared graham cracker crumbs or ⅔ cup flaked coconut.

Strawberry Squares

36 squares.

Utensils	Ingredients
Square baking pan,	½ cup butter or mar-
9 × 9 × 2 inches	garine (1 stick)
Large saucepan	3 cups miniature marsh-
Long-handled spoon	mallows or 32 large
Sharp knife	marshmallows
	½ cup instant nonfat
	dry milk
	½ cup strawberry-
	flavored quick milk
	mix
	4 cups O-shaped puffed
	oat cereal
	1 cup flaked coconut

1 Grease baking pan with some butter or margarine.

2 Heat ½ cup butter, 3 cups miniature marshmallows, ½ cup dry milk and ½ cup milk mix in saucepan over low heat until smooth, stirring constantly. Remove from heat.

3 Stir in 4 cups cereal and 1 cup coconut until coated. Empty into the buttered pan. Rub a little butter on the back of the spoon and use it to pat the mixture evenly in the pan. Cool. Cut into 1½-inch squares.

Sweets give you quick energy, but be careful not to eat too many—that extra energy can turn into fat. So when you feel like having a snack, don't forget the milk, cereal, fruit and vegetable snacks in this chapter. They're a wonderful way to include the foods you need every day.

Pictured: Cookie Ski Chalet (page 40) and Gumdrop Trees (page 42)

PARTIES
AND
PRESENTS

Chinese New Year

Fried Fortune Cookies

12 cookies.

Utensils	Ingredients
White paper	1 egg
Scissors	⅓ cup sugar
Pencil	⅓ cup all-purpose flour*
Griddle or electric skillet	3 tablespoons salad oil
Pastry brush	2 tablespoons water
Small bowl	½ teaspoon vanilla
Fork	¼ teaspoon cinnamon
Tablespoon	(if you like)
Pancake turner	
Small plate	
1 or 2 muffin pans	

1 Cut paper into strips about 3 inches long and ½ inch wide. Write a different fortune on each strip. (Examples: "You will have a happy day." "You will make a new friend soon.")

2 Heat griddle over medium heat (350° on electric skillet). Generously grease the hot griddle with shortening, using pastry brush.

3 Beat 1 egg in bowl with fork until foamy. Beat in ⅓ cup sugar until light and fluffy. Stir in ⅓ cup flour, 3 tablespoons

oil, 2 tablespoons water, ½ teaspoon vanilla and ¼ teaspoon cinnamon and mix until smooth.

4 Drop the batter by tablespoonfuls onto the greased hot griddle. Spread into circles about 3½ inches across, using the back of the spoon. (The cookies must be very thin.)

5 Cook until light brown, about 3 minutes. (Lift an edge and peek.) Turn with pancake turner and cook about 3 minutes on the other side.

6 Lift the cookies, one at a time, onto plate. Place a paper fortune in center of each cookie, then fold the cookie in half. Holding the edges, draw the cookie gently down over the edge of muffin pan to crease in half. Fit the cookie into a muffin pan cup to hold its shape until cool.

* Do not use self-rising flour in this recipe.

Note: These cookies need a flat surface for baking because the batter is so thin. If you use a slanted or warped griddle, they'll run all over the place! It's a good idea to brush a little oil on your pancake turner before you turn the first cookie.

For crisp fortune cookies, make them on a dry day, be sure the griddle is hot enough, grease the griddle with a thin coat of shortening and make sure to spread the batter very thin.

Valentine's Day

No-Cook Cherry Divinity

60 to 72 candies.

Utensils	Ingredients
Small saucepan	½ cup water
Small mixer bowl	1 package (7.7 ounces) fluffy cherry frosting mix
Electric mixer	
Rubber scraper	
Large mixer bowl	⅓ cup light corn syrup
Spoon	1 teaspoon vanilla
Teaspoon	1 package (16 ounces) powdered sugar (about 4½ cups)
Waxed paper	
	1 cup chopped nuts

1 Heat ½ cup water just to boiling in saucepan over medium-high heat. Pour the boiling water into small mixer bowl. Add the frosting mix, ⅓ cup corn syrup and 1 teaspoon vanilla. (You'll use the cherry bits from the package of frosting mix later.)

2 Beat on high speed until stiff peaks form, about 5 minutes. Turn off the mixer occasionally and scrape the side of the bowl.

3 Empty the mixture into large mixer bowl and gradually beat in the powdered sugar on low speed.

4 Stir in 1 cup chopped nuts and the cherry bits. Drop the mixture by teaspoonfuls about 1 inch apart onto waxed paper. Let stand until the surface of the candies feels firm, then turn them over and let stand at least 12 hours to dry.

Note: You can store leftover candy in a container with a tight cover at room temperature or freeze in the container as long as 2 months.

Cook's Corner

Why don't you make a Heart Cake for Valentine's Day? Heat the oven to 350°. Grease and flour 1 square baking pan, 8x8x2 inches, and 1 round layer pan, 8x1½ inches. Prepare 1 package (18.5 ounces) white cake mix as directed except—pour the batter into the pans, making sure both are filled to an equal depth. Bake the square layer 25 to 30 minutes and the round layer 30 to 35 minutes or until a wooden pick inserted in the center comes out clean. Cool the layers as directed.

Place the square layer on a large tray with 1 point toward you. Cut the round layer in half. Place the cut edge of each half against the top edges of the square to make a heart.

Prepare 1 package (7.7 ounces) cherry fluff frosting mix as directed and frost the Heart Cake, using a spatula. Decorate the cake or spell out a Valentine message with cinnamon candies, or sprinkle the cake with flaked coconut.

Easter

Chocolate Bunnies or Chicks

Pictured on page 133.

About 5 bunnies or chicks.

Utensils	Ingredients
Cookie sheet	1 package (6 ounces)
Waxed paper	semisweet chocolate
Small saucepan	chips
Long-handled spoon	1 tablespoon shortening
Bunny or chick cookie	Tiny colored candies
cutter	

1 Cover cookie sheet with waxed paper.

2 Heat the chocolate chips and 1 tablespoon shortening in saucepan over low heat until chocolate chips melt, stirring constantly.

3 Spread the chocolate mixture in a 6-inch square about ¼ inch thick on the waxed paper. Sprinkle generously with candies. Refrigerate 10 minutes. Cut out chocolate figures with cookie cutter.

4 Refrigerate 30 minutes or until firm. (The cook gets to eat the scraps!)

5 Use bunnies or chicks to decorate a frosted cake or press each one onto a sugar cookie or a graham cracker. If you like, stick them on with a little dab of canned frosting.

Noodle Nests

16 nests.

Utensils	Ingredients
Cookie sheet	1 can (16½ ounces)
Waxed paper	you favorite flavor
Large saucepan	frosting
Long-handled spoon	4 cups chow mein
	noodles
	Small jelly beans

1 Cover cookie sheet with waxed paper.

2 Heat the frosting in saucepan over low heat until frosting is liquid, stirring occasionally. Remove from heat.

3 Stir in 4 cups chow mein noodles until coated. Drop the mixture by ¼ cupfuls about 1 inch apart onto the waxed paper. Make a hollow in the center of each, using the back of the spoon. Does it look like a nest? Fill with jelly beans (3 to 5 for each nest). Let stand until firm.

You can make a nest full of eggs to decorate the top of a cupcake, a large cookie or a round cake. Frost the cupcake, cookie or cake (use canned frosting if you like). While the frosting is still sticky, press on some white or pastel-colored coconut and some tiny jelly beans. There—it's springtime!

HALLOWEEN

Little Pumpkin Cups

12 cups.

Utensils
1 or 2 muffin pans
12 paper baking cups
Large mixer bowl
Electric mixer
Rubber scraper

Ingredients
2 envelopes (about 1½
ounces each) whipped
topping mix
1 cup milk
1 teaspoon vanilla
1 teaspoon cinnamon
½ teaspoon salt
¼ teaspoon cloves
¼ teaspoon ginger
¼ teaspoon nutmeg
½ can (16-ounce size)
pumpkin (about 1
cup)
Candy corn

1 Line 12 muffin cups with baking cups. Prepare the topping mix as directed on envelopes, using a total of 1 cup milk and 1 teaspoon vanilla except—add 1 teaspoon cinnamon, ½ teaspoon salt, ¼ teaspoon cloves, ¼ teaspoon ginger and ¼ teaspoon nutmeg before beating. Fold in the pumpkin with rubber scraper.

2 Divide the mixture among the paper-lined muffin cups. Decorate each serving with candy corn. Refrigerate as long as 2 hours or freeze as long as 8 hours and remove to refrigerator 1 hour before serving.

Golden Pumpkin Loaf

Utensils
Pastry brush
Loaf pan, 9 × 5 × 3
inches
Large mixer bowl
Electric mixer
Wooden pick
Wire cooling rack

Ingredients
1 cup sugar
1 egg
1 can (16 ounces)
pumpkin
3 cups biscuit baking
mix
1 teaspoon pumpkin pie
spice
½ teaspoon cloves
½ teaspoon nutmeg

1 Heat oven to 350°. Generously grease loaf pan with shortening, using pastry brush.

2 Beat 1 cup sugar, 1 egg and the pumpkin in mixer bowl on medium speed 30 seconds. Gradually beat in remaining ingredients on low speed just until smooth. Pour into the greased pan.

3 Bake at 350° 1 hour and 10 minutes or until wooden pick inserted in center comes out clean.

4 Cool the pumpkin loaf 10 minutes on rack, then remove from the pan. Serve warm or cold.

Ghost Cake with Flaming Eyes

Utensils

Pastry brush
Oblong baking pan,
   13 × 9 × 2 inches
Large mixer bowl
Electric mixer
Rubber scraper
Wooden picks
Wire cooling rack
Tray, 16 × 12 inches,
   breadboard or
   aluminum foil-covered
   cardboard
Ruler
Small mixer bowl
Sharp knife
Spatula

Ingredients

1 package (18.5 ounces)
   yellow cake mix
1⅓ cups water
2 eggs
1 package (7.2 ounces)
   fluffy white frosting
   mix
1 cup water
2 sugar cubes
Licorice string
1 teaspoon lemon
   extract

1 Heat oven to 350°. Generously grease baking pan with shortening, using pastry brush. Sprinkle a little flour into the pan and shake gently from side to side until flour coats the bottom and sides. Empty out remaining flour.

2 Prepare the cake mix as directed on package. (When you break the eggs, crack each in the middle and pour out the egg. Then save the 2 best shell halves. Wash these halves and turn upside down to dry.) After mixing, pour the batter into the greased and floured pan.

3 Bake in 350° oven 35 to 40 minutes or until wooden pick inserted in the center comes out clean. Cool the cake 10 minutes on rack, then remove from the pan to tray.

4 After the cake is cool, measure across one short edge of the cake and mark the center with a wooden pick. Measure 4 inches down each long edge and mark with picks. Prepare the frosting as directed on package.

5 Cut the cake between the center wooden pick and side picks in a curve to make a rounded top for the ghost's head. Slide the cut corners down the sides to about the center of the cake. Turn the corners so the cut sides are up, to make arms that look as if they're reaching out for you. Attach the arms to the sides of the cake with some of the frosting, using spatula.

6 Frost the cake with the spatula. Place the 2 egg shell halves round sides down on cake for eyes. Place 1 sugar cube in each shell half. Make a mouth of licorice string.

7 Just before serving, pour ½ teaspoon lemon extract over each sugar cube. Ask someone older to light them for you. Lights off—it'll be spooky!

Cook's Corner

Bubble, bubble, toil and trouble—stir this brew up on the double! To make a cauldronful of Foaming Witches' Brew, cover the outside of a large kettle with black paper and tape it in place. Or ask someone older to help you scoop out a pumpkin, then line it with aluminum foil. Just before serving, fill the kettle or foil-lined pumpkin with chilled root beer and drop scoops of vanilla ice cream on top. Stir and serve right away. (For less ghostly occasions, pour strawberry-flavored soda pop into a big bowl and drop in scoops of your favorite flavor sherbet.)

Christmas

Cookie Ski Chalet
Pictured on page 33.

Utensils

2 medium bowls
Long-handled spoon
2 cookie sheets
Breadboard and
  pastry cloth
Rolling pin and
  stockinet cover
Custard cup
Ruler
Table knife
Pancake turner
Wire cooling rack
Wooden picks
Cookie cutters
Aluminum foil or tray,
  15 inches across
Brown paper
Spatula
Paintbrush (if you like)
Small bowl
Fork

Ingredients

2 packages (14.5 ounces
  each) gingerbread
  mix
⅓ cup water
⅓ cup more water
2 cans (16½ ounces
  each) vanilla frosting
Candy-coated chocolate
  candies
1-inch pieces of
  thick licorice
Large marshmallows
¼ cup water
Powdered sugar

1 Mix 1 package gingerbread mix and ⅓ cup water in medium bowl. Mix the second package and ⅓ cup water in another medium bowl. (Do not mix both packages at once.) Cover both bowls and refrigerate at least 2 hours.

2 When the dough has been refrigerated at least 2 hours, heat oven to 375°. Grease cookie sheets with shortening.

3 Cover breadboard with pastry cloth, tucking ends underneath. Cover rolling pin with stockinet cover. For convenience, place some flour in custard cup. Sprinkle the covered board and rolling pin generously with the flour and rub it in until it disappears.

4 Take out 1 bowl of dough. Roll the dough into a rectangle, 14 inches long, 11 inches wide and ¼ inch thick on the covered board. Cut away any uneven edges and save for rerolling.

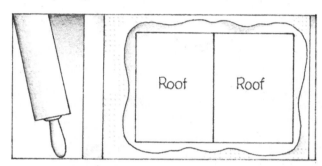

5 Cut the rectangle in half so you have 2 small rectangles, 11 inches long and 7 inches wide. Gently roll the rectangles onto the rolling pin, then lift to a greased cookie sheet and unroll.

6 Bake in 375° oven about 12 minutes. Loosen the rectangles slightly with pancake turner. Let cool 1 to 2 minutes, then carefully slide onto rack.

7 Take out the second bowl of dough. Roll the dough into a rectangle, 15 inches long, 10 inches wide and ¼ inch thick. Cut out a 10-inch square from the rectangle. Lift off the scraps of dough around the square with the pancake turner. (Save the scraps to roll again.)

8 Gently roll the square onto the rolling pin, then lift to the second greased cookie sheet and unroll. Measure 1 edge of the square and make a mark in the center with a wooden pick. Cut from this point to the 2 opposite corners. (If the triangles bake together, recut while warm.)

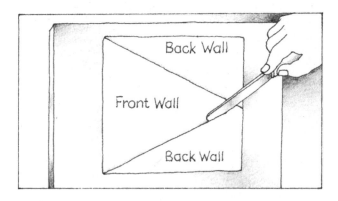

9 Bake in 375° oven about 12 minutes or until the edges are brown. Loosen, cool and remove to the rack as you did before. Cool the walls and roof of your chalet 1 hour.

10 While the walls and roof are cooling, use the scraps to cut out a door, 2½ inches long and 2 inches wide; 2 windows, each 3 inches long and 2½ inches wide; a round window, 1½ inches across; some skis (2 strips of gingerbread, each with a pointed end); and a deer or whatever you like. Bake the skis 6 to 8 minutes and the remaining pieces 8 to 10 minutes. Loosen, cool and

remove to the rack as you did before except—turn up the pointed ends of the skis while they're still warm. Then clean up all the dishes and get ready for the real fun—putting your chalet together.

To Put Your Chalet Together

1 Cover the breadboard with aluminum foil or use a tray.

2 Measure and cut out a rectangle, 9½ inches long and 5½ inches wide, of brown paper. Attach the paper to the middle of the board (or weight it on the tray). Spread some of the frosting from the first can on the board around the paper with spatula, touching but not covering the edge of the paper, in an outline ¾ inch wide and ¼ inch high. Lift off the paper and throw it away.

3 Spread some frosting on one short (7-inch) edge of each cookie rectangle. Stick these edges together. (They make the peak of the roof.) Press the bottom edges of the rectangles into the frosting on the board. Add extra frosting if you need it to hold the rectangles securely. Now you have the roof of your chalet.

4 Frost all the edges of the biggest cookie triangle. Ease it under the A-frame roof until there is 1 inch of roof overhanging the wall. Press roof gently against the wall to make sure everything is secure.

5 Put the edges of the other 2 triangles together with frosting to make a triangle like the first one, then frost all the edges. Ease under the A-frame roof to complete your chalet. (This may take 4 hands—2 to ease and 2 to hold the roof.) Let stand about 20 minutes so the frosting becomes firm. (If there is a gap at the peak of your roof, cut a piece of cardboard to cover it and frost over the cardboard.)

To Trim Your Chalet

1 Frost the back side of each door and window and press them onto the outside of the walls (the door and 2 windows go in front, and 1 window goes in back). Let stand 10 minutes, then "paint" on window panes with a wooden pick or paintbrush dipped in frosting. Stick decorations on with dabs of frosting. Here's a suggestion: candy-coated chocolate candies around the windows and licorice under the overhanging roof (see picture) for beams.

2 Spread remaining frosting from the first can on the board to make snow. Stick large marshmallows in it for hills. Lean the skis against the walls of the chalet and stand other cookie figures in the frosting if you like. (You can outline the skis with a wooden pick dipped in frosting if you like.)

3 Empty the second can of frosting into small bowl. Stir in ¼ cup water with fork. Frost the roof and marshmallow hills. Sprinkle some powdered sugar over the snow.

Try this cookie house as a team project for the entire family. It's much more fun, and you'll have lots of hands to help fit it together.

If the weather is very damp when you make your ski chalet, bake the walls and roof a few minutes longer than the recipe calls for. Then store the cookie pieces overnight in the turned-off (cool) oven. This will keep them from picking up any dampness from the air and getting soggy.

Gumdrop Trees

Pictured on page 33.

6 trees.

Utensils	Ingredients
Cookie sheet	4 cups O-shaped puffed
Large bowl	oat cereal
Large saucepan	32 large marshmallows
Long-handled spoon	or 3 cups miniature
Kitchen scissors	marshmallows
Glass	3 tablespoons butter or
	margarine
	½ teaspoon vanilla
	½ teaspoon green food
	color
	Small gumdrops

1 Grease cookie sheet with some butter or margarine.

2 Empty 4 cups cereal into bowl.

3 Heat 32 large marshmallows and 3 tablespoons butter in saucepan over medium heat until the marshmallows melt. Stir until smooth. Remove from heat. Stir in ½ teaspoon vanilla and ½ teaspoon food color.

4 Pour the marshmallow mixture over the cereal and stir until the cereal is coated.

5 Rub some butter on your hands and divide the cereal mixture into 6 parts on the greased cookie sheet, using about ⅔ cup for each. Shape each part into a tree shape.

6 Cut the gumdrops into slices with scissors. (Dip the scissors into glass of water to keep the candy from sticking.) Press the gumdrop slices onto the trees.

Birthday Ice-Cream Cake

About 12 servings.

Utensils	Ingredients
Shallow pan	½-gallon pail spumoni
Long spatula	(or your favorite
Serving plate	flavor) ice cream
Teaspoon	2½ cups frozen whipped
Candles	topping, thawed*
Candle holders	½ cup chocolate caramel
Sharp knife	sauce
Glass	

1 Fill pan almost to the top with warm water.

2 Remove cover from the pail of ice cream. Run spatula around inside of the pail to loosen the ice cream. Dip the pail quickly into the pan of warm water to loosen the ice cream. Place serving plate on top of the pail and turn pail over so the ice cream can slide out onto the plate. Lift off the pail. Place the ice cream in freezer immediately. Freeze about 1 hour or until firm.

3 Frost the ice cream with 2½ cups whipped topping, using the spatula.

4 Drizzle ½ cup chocolate caramel sauce in a circle around the top edge of the cake with teaspoon. Freeze until serving time.

5 Place candles in holders and arrange on top of the cake. Ask someone older for help in lighting the candles. To serve, cut the cake into wedges. (Dip the knife into glass of water for easier cutting.)

* This is a little more than half of a 9-ounce carton.

Note: In place of the pail of ice cream, you can use a ½-gallon brick of ice cream—just peel off the sides of the carton and lift the block of ice cream to a plate. Frost as directed above. In place of the frozen whipped topping, you can use 1 envelope (about 2 ounces) dessert topping mix, prepared as directed on envelope.

Bouncing Ball Punch

Pictured on page 59.

About 2 quarts punch.

Utensils	Ingredients
Punch bowl	3 packages (10 ounces
Long-handled spoon	each) frozen melon
	balls
	1 can (46 ounces)
	your favorite fruit
	punch drink
	1 can (6 ounces) frozen
	lemonade concentrate
	Water

1 About 40 minutes before you want to serve punch, remove the frozen melon balls from freezer. Let stand at room temperature about 20 minutes for easier opening.

2 Mix the fruit punch drink, lemonade concentrate and two 6-ounce cans water (use the lemonade can) in punch bowl. Add the frozen melon balls and let stand 15 minutes. Stir and serve.

Big Burger Cake

Utensils

Pastry brush
1½-quart round glass
 casserole
Small mixer bowl
Electric mixer
Rubber scraper
Wooden picks
Wire cooling rack
Serving plate
Cookie sheet
Ruler
Long serrated knife
Spatula
Small bowl
Spoon

Ingredients

1 package (16 ounces)
 golden pound cake
 mix
⅔ cup water
2 eggs
1 tablespoon sesame
 seeds
Easy Penuche Frosting
 (facing page)
2 tablespoons cocoa
2 tablespoons straw-
 berry preserves

1 Heat oven to 300°. Generously grease casserole with shortening, using pastry brush. Sprinkle a little flour into the casserole and shake gently from side to side until the flour coats the bottom and side. Empty out remaining flour.

2 Prepare the cake mix as directed on package except—after mixing, pour the batter into the greased and floured casserole.

3 Bake in 300° oven 1 hour and 5 to 10 minutes or until wooden pick inserted in the center comes out clean. Cool the cake on rack 10 minutes, then remove from the casserole to plate. Place the cake rounded side up.

4 While the cake is cooling, sprinkle 1 tablespoon sesame seeds on ungreased cookie sheet. Bake in 300° oven about 5 minutes or until golden. (You will use the seeds later to sprinkle over your cake.)

5 Prepare Easy Penuche Frosting.

6 After the cake is cool, you are going to cut it into 3 parts—1 for the top of the bun, 1 for the hamburger and 1 for the bottom of the bun. To do this, mark the cake for easier cutting by sticking wooden picks in the cake to guide your knife. Place 1 row of wooden picks (about 2 inches apart) 1 inch from the bottom of the cake and another row 2 inches from the bottom.

7 Using the wooden picks as a guide, slice off the top of the cake with serrated knife. This is easier if your eyes are at the same level as the cake, so bend down or put the cake on a high counter. Lift off the top and set aside. Cut off the next layer and set aside.

8 Frost the bottom layer with spatula.

9 Measure ⅓ cup of the remaining frosting into bowl and stir in 2 tablespoons cocoa. If the frosting seems stiff, stir in ½ teaspoon water. Place the middle (hamburger) layer on top of the bottom layer. Frost the middle layer with the cocoa-flavored frosting.

10 Place the top (rounded) layer on top of the middle layer. Frost with remaining frosting.

11 Drizzle 2 tablespoons preserves around the side of the middle layer to look like catsup.

12 Sprinkle the top of the cake with the toasted sesame seeds.

Easy Penuche Frosting

Utensils	Ingredients
Square baking pan, 8 × 8 × 2 or 9 × 9 × 2 inches	½ cup butter or margarine (1 stick)
Medium saucepan	1 cup brown sugar (packed)
Long-handled spoon	¼ cup milk
	2 cups powdered sugar

1 Fill baking pan about ⅓ of the way to the top with cold water and ice cubes. Melt ½ cup butter in saucepan over low heat. Stir in 1 cup brown sugar. Cook over low heat 2 minutes, stirring occasionally. Stir in ¼ cup milk. Heat to rolling boil, stirring constantly.

2 Remove from heat and set the saucepan in the pan of cold water and ice. When you can comfortably hold your hand on the bottom of the saucepan, gradually stir in 2 cups powdered sugar.

3 Place the saucepan back in the pan of ice water and beat the sugar mixture until it becomes thick enough to spread. If the frosting is too thin, add more powdered sugar. If it is too thick, add a few drops of hot water. Now go back to Step 6 of the cake recipe and follow the directions that tell you how to cut the cake into thirds, frost the layers and end up with a Big Burger Cake.

Pink Elephant Meringues

7 elephants.

Utensils	Ingredients
2 cookie sheets	3 eggs
Heavy brown paper	¼ teaspoon cream of
Small mixer bowl	tartar
Small bowl	¾ cup sugar
Electric mixer	¼ teaspoon red food
Rubber scraper	color
Teaspoon	7 miniature chocolate
Tablespoon	chips
Ice-cream scoop	1 quart vanilla, straw-
or large spoon	berry or chocolate
	ice cream

1 Heat oven to 275°. Cover cookie sheets with heavy brown paper.

2 Separate the whites from the yolks of 3 eggs.* Pour the whites into mixer bowl. Cover the yolks tightly in small bowl and refrigerate. Use within 1 or 2 days.

3 Add ¼ teaspoon cream of tartar to the egg whites and beat on high speed just until foamy.

4 Gradually beat in ¾ cup sugar, 1 tablespoon at a time. Turn off the mixer occasionally and scrape side of the bowl. Add ¼ teaspoon food color and continue beating on high speed until stiff and glossy, 7 to 8 minutes. Now you have an unbaked meringue.

5 For each elephant's body, scoop out ¼ cup of the meringue and push it onto the brown paper with rubber scraper. (Place 3 mounds on one cookie sheet and 4 on the other, leaving plenty of room around each mound.) Shape each mound into a circle about 2½ inches across with the back of the teaspoon, building up the side to make a hollow in the center. (This is where the ice cream goes later.)

6 For each elephant's head, drop a heaping tablespoonful of the meringue onto the brown paper, just touching the body. Shape into a circle.

7 For each trunk, floppy ear, tail and leg, drop about a teaspoonful of the meringue onto the brown paper, just touching the body. Shape with the back of the teaspoon. Does it look like an elephant? If you have leftover meringue, make each elephant a little fatter. If you run out of meringue, scoop a little from one elephant and add to another.

8 Place 1 chocolate chip on each elephant's head to make an eye.

9 Bake in 275° oven 45 minutes. Turn off the oven. Leave the meringues in the oven with the door closed 1 hour. Remove from oven.

10 Just before serving, fill each meringue body with a scoop of the ice cream. Serve right away.

* To separate an egg, see pages 138–139.

Shape each elephant's body by building up the sides of the meringue circle to make a hollow in the center.

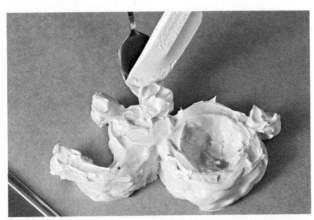
Make the elephant's head, trunk, ears, tail and legs with more meringue.

Fill each baked meringue elephant with a scoop of ice cream, then serve right away.

Popcorn Ring Centerpiece

1 ring.

Utensils	Ingredients
Pastry brush	7 cups popped corn
6-cup ring mold	½ cup brown sugar
Large bowl	(packed)
Small saucepan	¼ cup butter or mar-
Long-handled spoon	garine (½ stick)
Spatula	2 tablespoons light corn
Serving plate	syrup
Tall fat candle	¼ teaspoon salt
	¼ teaspoon baking soda

1 Generously grease ring mold with shortening, using pastry brush.

2 Empty 7 cups popped corn into bowl.

3 Heat ½ cup brown sugar, ¼ cup butter, 2 tablespoons corn syrup and ¼ teaspoon salt in saucepan over medium heat until bubbly around the edge, stirring constantly. Cook without stirring 4 minutes.

4 Remove from heat. Stir in ¼ teaspoon baking soda (this will make it foamy). Drizzle over the popped corn. Stir until the corn is coated.

5 Press the popcorn mixture into the greased ring mold with your hands. Let stand about 1 hour or until dry.

6 Just before serving, run spatula around the edges of the mold. Turn the mold on its side and hit its edge sharply on a countertop. Turn the popcorn ring over onto plate. Place candle in the center of the ring. When you've used your centerpiece and you're ready to eat the ring, lift out the candle and break off chunks of popcorn.

Gifts from the Kitchen

Creamy Caramels

Pictured on page 50.

64 caramel squares.

Utensils	Ingredients
Square baking pan, 8 × 8 × 2 inches	1 package (14.3 ounces) butter pecan frosting mix
Medium saucepan	½ cup butter or margarine (1 stick)
Long-handled spoon	1 cup light cream (20%)
Candy thermometer	½ cup light corn syrup
Glass	
Sharp knife	

1 Grease baking pan with some butter or margarine.

2 Mix the frosting mix, ½ cup butter, 1 cup light cream and ½ cup corn syrup in saucepan, stirring until just blended.

3 Cook without stirring over medium heat to 256° on candy thermometer or until a small amount of the mixture dropped into glass of very cold water forms a hard ball, about 30 minutes. Pour the mixture into the buttered pan. Refrigerate about 1 hour or until firm. Cut into 1-inch squares.

Homemade Crunchy Peanut Butter

1 cup peanut butter.

Utensils	Ingredients
Blender	2 cans (6½ ounces each) salted peanuts (2½ cups)
Rubber scraper	2 tablespoons butter or margarine, softened
Small bowl or jar	

1 Measure ½ cup of the peanuts. (You'll use them later.) Empty remaining peanuts (2 cups) into blender container. Cover and blend on low speed 10 seconds or until the peanuts are chopped.

2 Add 2 tablespoons butter to the chopped peanuts. Cover and blend on low speed 10 seconds. Turn off the blender, uncover and scrape down the sides with rubber scraper.

3 Cover and blend on low speed 5 seconds. Turn off the blender, uncover and scrape down the sides again. Repeat this step 3 or 4 times or until the peanut butter starts to get smooth. Cover and blend on highest speed 1 minute.

4 Uncover and add the ½ cup peanuts. Cover and blend on medium speed 3 seconds.

5 Empty the peanut butter into bowl. Refrigerate about 30 minutes.

VARIATION

Smooth Peanut Butter: Blend all 2½ cups peanuts in step 1. Then continue as above except—leave out step 4.

Rosy Grape Jelly

Pictured on page 50.

5 jars jelly.

Utensils	Ingredients
Five 7-ounce jars or glasses	2 cups cranberry juice
Kitchen towel	¾ cup grape juice
4-quart saucepan	1 package (1¾ ounces) powdered fruit pectin
Long-handled spoon	3¼ cups sugar
Jar lids or aluminum foil	

1 Wash jars in hot, soapy water. Rinse thoroughly and turn upside down on folded towel to drain. (The jars should be warm and dry when you fill them with jelly.)

2 Mix thoroughly 2 cups cranberry juice, ¾ cup grape juice and the pectin in saucepan. (There shouldn't be any lumps.) Heat to boiling over high heat, stirring constantly. Stir in 3¼ cups sugar all at once. Heat to boiling and boil 1 minute, stirring constantly.

3 Remove from heat and quickly skim off any bubbles. Ask someone older to pour the jelly into the jars for you, since it's very hot. (This should be done right away.)

4 Let jars stand 1 hour, then cover with lids. Refrigerate. (The jelly will keep as long as 3 weeks in the refrigerator or as long as 6 months in the freezer. To thaw frozen jelly, refrigerate or let stand at room temperature several hours.)

Note: This recipe will also fill seven 5-ounce glasses or eight 4½-ounce baby food jars. Any size or shape dishwasher-safe containers made of glass or plastic can be used.

Cook's Corner

Have you ever thought of giving homemade food gifts to your family and friends? They're very special presents because you make them yourself.

Part of the fun of making jelly is eating it—and another part is giving it away. When you give a jar as a present, it's nice to paste on a label you've made. Wrap the jar with bright tissue paper or a scrap of colorful cloth and fasten it with yarn or ribbon. Include a tag with instructions on how to store the jelly if you like.

Rocky Road Fudge

Pictured on page 50.

64 fudge squares.

Utensils	Ingredients
Square baking pan, 8 × 8 × 2 inches	¼ cup milk
Medium saucepan	2 packages (5¾ ounces each) milk chocolate chips
Long-handled spoon	2 cups miniature marshmallows
Spatula	½ cup chopped nuts
Table knife	Dash of salt

1 Grease baking pan with some butter or margarine.

2 Heat ¼ cup milk and the chocolate chips in saucepan over low heat until chocolate chips melt, stirring constantly.

3 Remove from heat. Stir in 2 cups miniature marshmallows, ½ cup chopped nuts and dash of salt. (The marshmallows will make little lumps in the candy.)

4 Spread the candy in the buttered pan with spatula. Refrigerate about 1 hour or until firm. Cut into 1-inch squares.

Caramel Apples

Pictured on the facing page.

6 apples.

Utensils	Ingredients
6 wooden ice-cream sticks	6 medium apples
Waxed paper	6 tablespoons granola or chopped salted peanuts
Double boiler or medium saucepan	1 package (14 ounces) vanilla caramels
Long-handled spoon	3 tablespoons water
	¼ cup creamy peanut butter
	½ teaspoon cinnamon

1 Wash 6 apples and poke an ice-cream stick in the stem end of each.

2 Using 1 tablespoon of granola for each mound, make 6 mounds of granola about 3 inches apart on waxed paper.

3 Heat the caramels, 3 tablespoons water, ¼ cup peanut butter and ½ teaspoon cinnamon in top of double boiler over hot water until caramels melt and the mixture is smooth, about 20 minutes, stirring frequently.

4 Remove from heat. (Keep the top of the double boiler over the hot water.)

5 Dip each apple in the hot caramel mixture and spoon mixture over the apple until it is completely coated. Hold the apple right side up by the stick for a second, then place it stick side up on one of the mounds of granola. Turn the apple so all the granola sticks to it.

6 Refrigerate about 1 hour or until the caramel coating is firm.

Pictured: Rosy Grape Jelly, Gumdrop Squares, Caramel Apple, Frosted Pretzels, Creamy Caramels, Rocky Road Fudge, Peppermint Taffy (pages 48-52)

Gumdrop Squares

Pictured on the facing page.

About 45 squares.

Utensils	Ingredients
Medium saucepan	1⅓ cups applesauce
Long-handled spoon	2 envelopes unflavored gelatin
Loaf pan, 9 × 5 × 3 inches	1 package (6 ounces) your favorite fruit-flavored gelatin
Rubber scraper	2 cups sugar
Table knife	1 teaspoon bottled lemon juice
Glass	Sugar
Cookie sheet	
Small bowl	

1 Mix 1⅓ cups applesauce, the unflavored gelatin, fruit-flavored gelatin, 2 cups sugar and 1 teaspoon lemon juice in saucepan. Heat to boiling and boil 1 minute, stirring frequently.

2 Fill loaf pan halfway to the top with cold water. Pour the water out, then immediately pour the gelatin mixture into the wet pan, using rubber scraper to clean the side of the saucepan.

3 When the loaf pan is cool enough to touch, refrigerate about 3 hours or until the candy is firm.

4 Cut the candy into 1-inch squares. (Dip the knife in glass of water to keep the candy from sticking.)

5 Lift each square from the pan onto ungreased cookie sheet. Let stand at least 8 hours to dry.

6 After the candy has dried, place some sugar in bowl, then roll each square in the sugar until all sides are coated.

Peppermint Taffy

Pictured on page 50.

About 1 pound taffy.

Utensils	Ingredients
2 square baking pans, 8 × 8 × 2 inches	1 cup sugar
Medium saucepan	¾ cup light corn syrup
Long-handled spoon	⅔ cup water
Candy thermometer	1 tablespoon cornstarch
Glass	2 tablespoons butter or margarine
Kitchen scissors	1 teaspoon salt
Plastic wrap	1 tablespoon peppermint extract
	8 to 10 drops red food color

1 Grease baking pans with some butter or margarine.

2 Heat all ingredients except the peppermint extract and food color just to boiling in saucepan over medium heat, stirring constantly. Cook without stirring to 256° on candy thermometer or until a small amount of the mixture dropped into glass of very cold water forms a hard ball, about 30 minutes.

3 Remove from heat and stir in 1 tablespoon peppermint extract. Pour half the mixture into one of the buttered pans. Stir 8 to 10 drops food color into remaining mixture, then pour into the other buttered pan. Let cool 15 to 20 minutes. (Ask for help from someone older in deciding when the taffy is cool enough to pull—it has to be cooled in the center and not just at the edges.)

4 When the taffy is ready to pull, wash and dry your hands and rub some butter on them.

5 Keep the 2 colors of taffy separate. Fold, double and pull each color of taffy until it is light in color and stiff. (Ask a brother, sister or friend to help.) If the taffy sticks, rub some more butter on your hands.

6 Pull each color of taffy into a long strip ½ inch wide, then put the 2 colors together and twist. Cut into 1- to 3-inch pieces with scissors. Shape the longer pieces into candy canes. (If the taffy becomes too hard to pull, heat it in a 350° oven a few minutes to soften it.)

7 Wrap each piece with plastic wrap. (Taffy will lose its shape if it isn't wrapped.)

Frosted Pretzels

Pictured on page 50.

15 pretzels.

Utensils	Ingredients
Rubber scraper	1 can (16½ ounces) vanilla frosting
Double boiler	15 pretzel twists
Long-handled spoon	
Waxed paper	

1 Measure 1 cup frosting. (Refrigerate remaining frosting for another time.)

2 Heat the 1 cup frosting in top of double boiler over hot water until frosting is liquid, stirring occasionally. Remove from heat. (Keep the top of the double boiler over the hot water.)

3 Dip 15 pretzel twists into the frosting with your fingers, then place them on waxed paper. Let dry 8 hours.

Pictured: Cheesy Skillet Drop Biscuits (page 62) and Grilled Bacon (page 56)

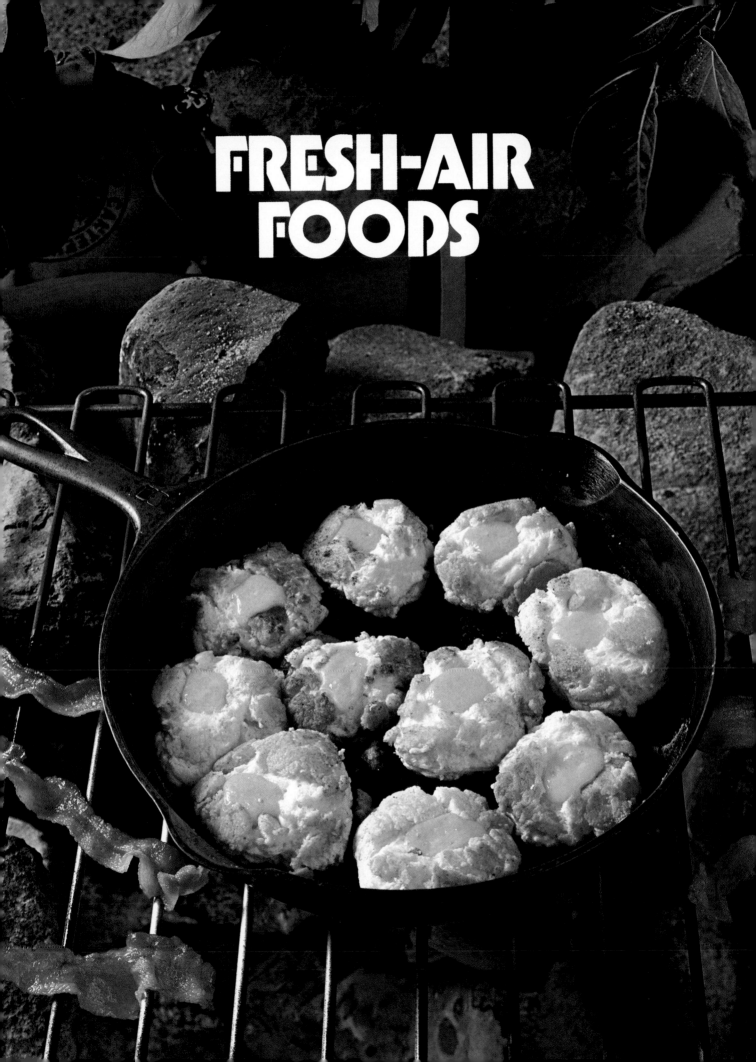

FRESH-AIR FOODS

Walking Salads

Wrap your walking salads in plastic bags, plastic wrap or aluminum foil. Then stop along the way for a quick pick-me-up.

1 Core an apple to within ½ inch of the bottom. Carve out the top slightly to make a little well about 1½ inches across. Fill the cavity with some cottage cheese. Pack a plastic fork with this salad. (You can scoop out and fill a tomato with cottage cheese too.)

2 Wrap a 4-inch slice of bologna around a pickle or a strip of cheese. Wrap the bologna with a tender cabbage leaf. Fasten with a wooden pick.

3 Fill some 4-inch celery stalks, washed and dried, with cream cheese, pineapple-cream cheese spread or your favorite cheese spread. Sprinkle with paprika—red ants on a log!

4 Fill some 4-inch celery stalks, washed and dried, with plain or crunchy peanut butter, then press in raisins here and there —bugs on a log!

5 Cut the peel from the top of an orange and make 4 cuts down the side—just through the skin but not into the juicy part —for easier peeling.

6 Make mini-kabobs on wooden picks. Here's a suggestion: cubes of cheese with drained pineapple chunks or maraschino cherries, or cubes of bologna with stuffed olives and pickle slices.

7 Pack a handful of vegetable snacks to quench your thirst: carrot curls, celery sticks, radishes and green pepper strips.

Chicken Noodle Soup

5 servings (about 1 cup each).

Utensils	Ingredients
Medium saucepan Long-handled spoon Kitchen scissors	2 cans (10¾ ounces each) condensed chicken broth Water 2¼ cups uncooked egg noodles (about half of 8-ounce package) 1 can (5 ounces) boned chicken 2 or 3 parsley sprigs

1 Ask someone older to light the charcoal and watch the fire. Adjust grill so it is 3 to 4 inches from hot coals.

2 Prepare the broth as directed on can except—heat to boiling on the grill. Stir in 2¼ cups noodles and the chicken. Cook the soup until the noodles are tender, 8 to 10 minutes.

3 Snip 2 or 3 parsley sprigs with scissors into the soup just before serving.

Note: In place of the can of chicken, you can use 1 cup cut-up cooked chicken.

Quick Soup with Rice

6 servings (1 cup each).

Utensils	Ingredients
Medium saucepan with cover Long-handled spoon	1 can (10¾ ounces) condensed tomato soup or 1 can (10½ ounces) condensed beef broth (bouillon) Water 1 cup uncooked instant rice

1 Ask someone older to light the charcoal and watch the fire. Adjust grill so it is 3 to 4 inches from hot coals.

2 Prepare the soup as directed on can except—heat to boiling on the grill. Stir in 1 cup rice. Cover and remove from heat.

3 Let stand 5 minutes before serving.

Note to outdoor cooks: The cooking time over an open fire varies, depending on how hot your fire is and how well it's controlled. So always cook food until it's done the way you like it.

Never heat canned foods in unopened cans! They can get so hot that they burst open. *Ouch!*

And here's a camping-out tip to remember: Bring along a length of clothesline. String it between 2 trees and use clothespins to hang up jackets, towels and sacks of food to keep them off the ground.

Potato-Egg Scramble

4 to 6 servings.

Utensils	Ingredients
Large skillet	3 slices bacon
Long-handled tongs	1 package (6 ounces)
Paper towel	hash browns with
Long-handled spoon	onions
Pancake turner	1¾ cups water
Small bowl	1 teaspoon salt
Fork	4 eggs
	½ teaspoon salt
	Dash of pepper

1 Ask someone older to light the charcoal and watch the fire. Adjust grill so it is 3 to 4 inches from hot coals.

2 Cook 3 slices bacon in skillet until crisp as directed in Grilled Bacon (right). Drain the bacon on paper towel. Spoon out most of the fat and throw it away, leaving just enough to cover the bottom of the skillet.

3 Mix the hash browns with onions, 1¾ cups water and 1 teaspoon salt in the skillet. Cook uncovered on the grill until the liquid is absorbed and the bottom of the potatoes is golden brown. (Lift the edge with pancake turner and peek.) Turn the potatoes with the pancake turner.

4 While the potatoes are cooking, beat 4 eggs, ½ teaspoon salt and dash of pepper in bowl with fork.

5 Pour the egg mixture over the potatoes. Cook and stir until the eggs are thick but still moist.

6 Just before serving, crumble the bacon over the potato-egg mixture.

Grilled Bacon
Pictured on page 53.

Utensils	Ingredient
Large skillet	Bacon slices
Long-handled tongs	

1 Ask someone older to light the charcoal and watch the fire. Adjust grill so it is 3 inches from hot coals.

2 Cook bacon slices (as many as you need) in skillet on the grill 3 to 4 minutes on each side, turning with tongs. (How long you cook the bacon depends on how crisp you like it.)

3 If you like, the bacon can be cooked directly on the grill 3 to 4 minutes on each side.

Note: For rainy day bacon, stay home and cook it in the microwave oven if you have one. Place 4 layers of paper towels in a shallow baking dish. Place 4 slices bacon on the towels. Top with a layer of paper towels. Cook 3 to 5 minutes or until the bacon is as crisp as you like it.

Texas-Style Chili

4 servings.

Utensils	Ingredients
Large skillet with cover	1 pound ground beef
Long-handled spoon	1 can (15½ ounces) chili beans or kidney beans
	1 can (10¾ ounces) condensed tomato soup
	¼ teaspoon chili powder
	¼ teaspoon onion salt
	Dash of red pepper sauce

1 Ask someone older to light the charcoal and watch the fire. Adjust grill so it is 3 to 4 inches from hot coals.

2 Crumble the ground beef into skillet. Cook and stir on the grill until brown on all sides, about 10 minutes. Spoon out any extra fat and throw it away.

3 Stir the chili beans (with liquid) and soup into the ground beef. Stir in ¼ teaspoon chili powder, ¼ teaspoon onion salt and dash of red pepper sauce.

4 Cover the skillet and cook 20 minutes. Uncover and cook 5 to 10 minutes, stirring occasionally.

Cook's Corner

For a quick one-pot cookout dinner, use 1 pound of ground beef and a mix (7- or 8-ounce package) for noodle, macaroni or potato dinner. Brown and drain the ground beef as in Step 2 of Texas-Style Chili (left). Add the noodles, macaroni or potatoes, hot water and Sauce Mix and cook as directed on the package.

And for easier cleanup outdoors, rub the *outside* of each cooking pot or pan with soap or liquid detergent before you cook in it. The black soot will come right off!

Double Steak Sandwiches

4 sandwiches.

Utensils	Ingredients
Long-handled tongs	8 beef cubed steaks, ¼ inch thick
Sharp knife	4 Kaiser rolls
Table knife	Soft butter or margarine
	Garlic salt

1 Ask someone older to light the charcoal and watch the fire. Adjust grill so it is 2 inches from hot coals.

2 Cook the beef steaks on the grill about 3 minutes on each side, turning with tongs. (You may want to ask for another opinion in deciding when the steaks are cooked through.)

3 Cut 4 Kaiser rolls in half with sharp knife. Spread with butter, using table knife, and sprinkle with garlic salt.

4 Stack 2 steaks in each roll for a hearty sandwich.

Foot-Long Coneys

6 coneys.

Utensils	Ingredients
Medium saucepan	1 can (24 ounces) chili with beans
Long-handled spoon	
Sharp knife	1 can (6 ounces) tomato paste
Long-handled tongs	
Table knife or spatula	1 teaspoon prepared mustard
	½ teaspoon salt
	6 foot-long frankfurters
	Soft butter or margarine
	6 foot-long frankfurter buns

1 Ask someone older to light the charcoal and watch the fire. Adjust grill so it is 4 inches from hot coals.

2 Mix the chili, tomato paste, 1 teaspoon mustard and ½ teaspoon salt in saucepan. Cook on the grill until hot and bubbly, 10 to 12 minutes, stirring occasionally.

3 Make 3 or 4 diagonal cuts ¼ inch deep in each frankfurter. Cook the frankfurters on the grill about 3 minutes on each side, turning with tongs.

4 Just before serving, spread the frankfurter buns with soft butter. Toast buttered sides down on the grill. Watch carefully!

5 Serve the frankfurters in the toasted buns, topped with the hot chili mixture.

Note: There are about 6 foot-long frankfurters in 1 pound.

Can't find those foot-long hot dogs and buns? Use twice as many regular-size hot dogs and buns for the amount of filling in this recipe.

Frankabobs

10 kabobs.

Utensils	Ingredients
Cutting board	1 can (13¼ ounces) pineapple chunks
Sharp knife	
10 metal skewers, 8 inches long	10 frankfurters
Pastry brush	2 tablespoons salad oil
Long-handled tongs	

1 Ask someone older to light the charcoal and watch the fire. Adjust grill so it is about 4 inches from hot coals.

2 Drain the can of pineapple chunks.

3 Cut each frankfurter crosswise into 5 equal pieces on cutting board.

4 Place 1 frankfurter piece on each skewer, then 1 pineapple chunk, then 1 frankfurter piece and so on, until 5 frankfurter pieces and 4 pineapple chunks are on each skewer. Brush kabobs with 2 tablespoons oil.

5 Cook kabobs on the grill 5 minutes on each side, turning with tongs.

Note: You may want to save the drained pineapple syrup and add it to your morning orange juice or use it as part of the liquid for making fruit gelatin.

VARIATIONS

Potatobobs: In place of the pineapple chunks, use small canned potatoes. Sprinkle with salt and paprika before cooking.

Dillybobs: In place of the pineapple chunks, use dill pickle chunks.

Pictured: Potatobobs (above) and Bouncing Ball Punch (page 43)

Bean Weenie Dip

10 servings.

Utensils	Ingredients
Small saucepan	1 can (11½ ounces) condensed bean with bacon soup
Long-handled spoon	
Cutting board	
Sharp knife	1 can (8 ounces) tomato sauce
3 serving bowls	
Long-handled forks	1 teaspoon instant minced onion
	10 frankfurters
	4 slices white bread
	1 package (11 ounces) corn chips

1 Ask someone older to light the charcoal and watch the fire. Adjust grill so it is 3 to 4 inches from hot coals.

2 Heat the soup, tomato sauce and 1 teaspoon minced onion in saucepan on the grill just until heated through, stirring frequently.

3 While the soup mixture heats, cut the frankfurters crosswise into 1½-inch pieces on cutting board. Place in serving bowl. Tear 4 slices bread into 1½-inch pieces into another serving bowl. Empty the corn chips into another serving bowl.

4 Move the hot soup mixture to one side of the grill. Let everyone toast his or her own bread pieces and frankfurter pieces over the coals with long-handled forks and dip them and the corn chips into the hot soup mixture. (Safety tip: Transfer your hot frank and toast to another fork to cool them before you dip them.)

Quick Chix on Stix

6 servings.

Utensils	Ingredients
Large saucepan	1 can (16 ounces) French-style green beans
Long-handled spoon	
6 dinner plates	2 cans (5 ounces each) boned chicken
	1 can (10¾ ounces) condensed cream of mushroom soup
	4 cups chow mein noodles (about 8 ounces)

1 Ask someone older to light the charcoal and watch the fire. Adjust grill so it is 4 inches from hot coals.

2 Drain the cans of beans and chicken.

3 Mix the beans, chicken and soup in saucepan. Cook on the grill until hot and bubbly.

4 Place about ⅔ cup chow mein noodles on each plate. Serve the hot chicken mixture over the noodles.

Fish Cooked in Foil

4 servings.

Utensils	Ingredients
Cutting board	1 pound frozen skinless sole, haddock or flounder fillets
Sharp knife	
Four 8-inch squares heavy-duty aluminum foil	About 2 tablespoons salad oil
Pastry brush	1 lemon
Long-handled tongs	½ teaspoon salt
	½ teaspoon paprika
	1 tomato
	Salt
	Bacon-flavored vegetable protein chips or parsley sprigs (if you like)

1 Ask someone older to light the charcoal and watch the fire.

2 Let the frozen fillets stand at room temperature 10 minutes for easier cutting.

3 Cut the fillets into 4 blocks of equal size on cutting board.

4 Place each block in center of square of aluminum foil. Brush each block on both sides with about 1½ teaspoons oil.

5 Cut 4 slices from half of the lemon. (You'll use these later.) Squeeze juice from remaining half of the lemon over the blocks. Sprinkle each block with about ⅛ teaspoon salt and about ⅛ teaspoon paprika. Top with 1 lemon slice.

6 Wash and cut stem end from 1 tomato. Cut into 4 slices on cutting board. Place 1 tomato slice on each lemon slice. Sprinkle each tomato slice with a little salt.

7 Bring 2 sides of the foil up to meet above the food. Press the top edges of the foil together and make a series of folds until foil is close to the food. Crease the unfolded ends to points and fold under. Place the foil packets directly on the hot coals with tongs.

8 Cook 30 minutes. Open the foil carefully. Garnish with bacon-flavored chips.

Corn in the Coals

4 servings.

Utensils	Ingredients
Heavy-duty aluminum foil	4 ears sweet corn
Long-handled tongs	4 tablespoons butter or margarine (½ stick)
	4 ice cubes or 8 tablespoons water

1 Ask someone older to light the charcoal and watch the fire.

2 Remove husks and silk from 4 ears corn.

3 Place each ear in the center of sheet of aluminum foil (about 3 times as wide and 2 inches longer than the corn). Add 1 tablespoon butter or margarine and 1 ice cube (or about 2 tablespoons water) for each ear of corn.

4 Wrap each ear securely in the foil, twisting the ends to make handles for turning. Place the foil packets directly on the hot coals with tongs. Cook 10 to 15 minutes, depending on the size of the ears, turning once.

Cheesy Skillet Biscuits

10 biscuits.

Utensils	Ingredients
Breadboard	¼ cup butter or mar-
Large skillet with cover	garine (½ stick)
Medium bowl	Dash of onion salt
Fork	Dash of garlic salt
Biscuit cutter	Dash of paprika
Cutting board	2 cups biscuit baking
Sharp knife	mix
	½ cup water
	Block of Cheddar
	cheese, 2½ × 1 × ½
	inch

1 Ask someone older to light the charcoal and watch the fire. Adjust the grill so it is about 4 inches from hot coals.

2 Rub some flour into breadboard to cover about a 10-inch area.

3 Melt ¼ cup butter in skillet on the grill. Remove from the grill. Sprinkle the melted butter with dash of onion salt, dash of garlic salt and dash of paprika.

4 Mix 2 cups baking mix and ½ cup water to a soft dough in bowl with fork. Place on the floured board and knead 5 times. Pat the dough to a ½-inch thickness and cut out 10 biscuits. Arrange the biscuits in the skillet and turn with the fork to coat with the seasoned butter.

5 Cut the cheese into ½-inch cubes on cutting board. Press 1 cheese cube lightly into each biscuit.

6 Cover the skillet and place on the grill. Cook 5 minutes. Lift the cover and make sure the biscuits are not burning. (Lift one and peek.) Cover and cook 5 minutes more or until the tops of the biscuits are dry.

Note: Use a heavy skillet so that these buttery biscuits will be golden, not burned. If you don't have a cover, use heavy-duty aluminum foil.

VARIATIONS

Cheesy Skillet Drop Biscuits: Follow recipe for Cheesy Skillet Biscuits except—instead of rolling the dough, drop by spoonfuls into the skillet. *(Pictured on page 53.)*

Sugar Babies: Follow recipe for Cheesy Skillet Biscuits except—omit the onion salt, garlic salt and paprika. In place of the cheese, use 10 sugar cubes. Dip sugar cubes 1 at a time into a small bowl of orange juice and press 1 lightly into each biscuit. Cook as directed.

Orange you thirsty? If you are, try an Orange Sip: Poke a peppermint candy stick into an orange, then sip the juice through your sweet straw.

Herbed Bread in Foil

24 to 28 slices.

Utensils	Ingredients
Cutting board	1 loaf (1 pound) French bread
Sharp knife	½ cup soft butter or margarine
Heavy-duty aluminum foil	2 teaspoons parsley flakes
Small bowl	½ teaspoon oregano leaves
Spoon	2 tablespoons grated Parmesan cheese
Table knife	⅛ teaspoon garlic salt
Long-handled tongs	

1 Ask someone older to light the charcoal and watch the fire. Adjust grill so it is 3 to 4 inches from hot coals.

2 Cut the bread into 1-inch slices on cutting board. Place in the center of sheet of aluminum foil (about 3 times as wide and 3 inches longer than the loaf).

3 Mix ½ cup soft butter, 2 teaspoons parsley flakes, ½ teaspoon oregano leaves, 2 tablespoons grated cheese and ⅛ teaspoon garlic salt in bowl. Spread each bread slice generously with the seasoned butter.

4 Reassemble the loaf and wrap securely with the foil, twisting the ends to make handles for turning.

5 Heat on the grill 15 to 20 minutes, turning once with tongs.

Note: In place of the French bread, you can use 8 large club rolls, cut in half. Heat 10 to 12 minutes.

Mallow Apples in the Coals

6 apples.

Utensils	Ingredients
Apple corer	6 tart red apples
Sharp knife	6 vanilla caramels
Six 10-inch squares heavy-duty aluminum foil	24 miniature marshmallows
Long-handled tongs	6 teaspoons raisins
Spoon	1 snack-size can (5 ounces) vanilla pudding

1 Ask someone older to light the charcoal and watch the fire.

2 Wash and core 6 apples to within ½ inch of bottoms. Carve out the tops slightly to make little wells about 1½ inches across. Place each apple in the center of square of aluminum foil.

3 Fill each cavity with 1 caramel, 4 miniature marshmallows and 1 teaspoon raisins.

4 Bring the 4 points of each square of foil together at the top of each apple and twist to close securely. Place the foil packets directly on the hot coals with tongs.

5 Cook about 20 minutes or until soft. Open foil carefully. Serve warm, with a spoonful of the vanilla pudding over each apple.

Note: These are fun to cook when you're already cooking something else on the grill. Or try baking them (all wrapped in aluminum foil) on a jelly roll pan in a 350° oven for 45 to 60 minutes. Open the foil with caution— watch out for the steam!

S'More

1 serving.

Utensil	Ingredients
Pointed green stick or long-handled fork	4 sections of milk chocolate candy bar 2 square graham crackers 1 large marshmallow

1 Ask someone older to light the charcoal and watch the fire.

2 Place 4 sections of chocolate on 1 graham cracker. Poke pointed green stick through 1 large marshmallow.

3 Toast over the hot coals until the marshmallow is brown, then slip it onto the chocolate and top with remaining graham cracker. Eat like a sandwich. Want s'more?

Chocolate Milk

3 cups chocolate milk.

Utensil	Ingredients
1-quart container with cover	⅔ cup instant nonfat dry milk ¼ cup instant chocolate-flavored quick milk mix 2 cups cold water

Measure ⅔ cup dry milk, ¼ cup milk mix and 2 cups cold water into container. Shake to mix.

Note: This quick chocolate milk is delicious hot too. Cook in a saucepan on a prepared grill about 10 minutes or until hot, stirring frequently.

Caramel Fondue

4 to 6 servings.

Utensils	Ingredients
Small saucepan Long-handled spoon Long-handled forks or wooden picks	1 jar (12 ounces) caramel ice-cream topping Dippers (below)

1 Ask someone older to light the charcoal and watch the fire. Adjust grill so it is about 4 inches from hot coals.

2 Heat the ice-cream topping in saucepan on the grill just until heated through, stirring frequently.

3 Spear Dippers with long-handled forks and swirl in the fondue.

Dippers: Apple slices, banana chunks, doughnut pieces.

Campers' Foaming Soda Pop

1 serving.

Utensils	Ingredients
Tall glass Long-handled spoon	Your favorite carbonated soda pop 2 tablespoons instant nonfat dry milk

1 Fill glass ⅓ of the way to the top with soda pop. Stir in 2 tablespoons instant dry milk.

2 Serve right away, adding more soda pop as you need it.

Pictured: Frozen Dough Fun (page 83)

A BUNCH OF BREADS

Chunky Tuna Sandwiches

6 sandwiches.

Utensils	Ingredients
Medium bowl	1 can (6½ ounces) tuna
Cutting board	1 celery stalk
Sharp knife	1 large kosher dill pickle
Fork	¼ cup mayonnaise or salad dressing
Table knife or spatula	¼ teaspoon onion salt
	¼ teaspoon bottled lemon juice
	12 slices white or whole wheat bread
	Soft butter or margarine

1 Drain the can of tuna, then place the tuna in bowl.

2 Wash 1 celery stalk and pinch off leaves. Chop the celery and 1 pickle into ¼-inch pieces on cutting board. Place in the bowl with the tuna.

3 Stir in ¼ cup mayonnaise, ¼ teaspoon onion salt and ¼ teaspoon lemon juice with fork.

4 Spread 12 slices bread with soft butter, then spread half of them with the tuna mixture and cover with remaining slices to make 6 sandwiches. Refrigerate any leftovers.

VARIATION

Hot Tuna Sandwiches: Follow recipe for Chunky Tuna Sandwiches except—heat oven to 375°. In place of the bread, use 3 hamburger buns, cut in half. Place the halves on an ungreased cookie sheet. Omit the butter. Spread each bun half with about 1/6 of the tuna mixture. Wash and cut stem end from 1 medium tomato. Cut it into 6 slices on the cutting board. Place 1 slice on each bun half and sprinkle with a little salt. Cover each tomato slice with 1 slice process American cheese and sprinkle with a little paprika. Bake in 375° oven 8 minutes or until the cheese melts.

Hard-cooked eggs are very easy to make, and there are lots of things you can do with them: You need them for the Egg Salad-Peanut Sandwiches on the facing page. A hard-cooked egg and a tiny saltshaker packed in a pocket when you go out for a hike makes a terrific snack. Or pop one into your lunch box for some extra protein power. You can refrigerate hard-cooked eggs for up to 7 days, so make a few to have around for when you want them.

To prepare hard-cooked eggs, place as many eggs as you want to cook in a saucepan with a cover. Add enough cold water to come at least 1 inch above the eggs. Heat to boiling over medium-high heat. Remove from the heat and cover. Let stand 22 to 24 minutes.

Uncover the saucepan and place it in the sink. Run cold water into the pan to cool the eggs quickly. (This makes the eggs easier to shell and keeps the yolks from turning dark around the edges.)

To shell the eggs, tap each one on the kitchen counter to crack the shell. Roll it between your hands to loosen the shell. Hold it under cold water as you peel it.

Egg Salad-Peanut Sandwiches

4 sandwiches.

Utensils	Ingredients
Cutting board	3 hard-cooked eggs*
Sharp knife	1 celery stalk
Medium bowl	¼ cup salted peanuts
Spoon	3 tablespoons mayon-
Table knife	naise or salad
	dressing
	¼ teaspoon onion salt
	⅛ teaspoon salt
	Soft butter or margarine
	8 slices rye or whole
	wheat bread

1 Peel 3 hard-cooked eggs.

2 Wash 1 celery stalk and pinch off leaves. (Keep them to feed the gerbils or add to a salad for decoration.)

3 Chop the celery and ¼ cup peanuts into very small pieces and the eggs into ¼-inch pieces on cutting board. Place in bowl.

4 Stir in 3 tablespoons mayonnaise, ¼ teaspoon onion salt and ⅛ teaspoon salt.

5 Spread 8 slices bread with soft butter, then spread half of them with the egg mixture and cover with remaining slices to make 4 sandwiches. Cut each sandwich in half and serve right away. Refrigerate any leftover sandwiches.

* To hard-cook eggs, see the facing page.

VARIATION

Egg Salad Sandwiches: Follow recipe for Egg Salad-Peanut Sandwiches except—omit the peanuts.

Baked Cheese Sandwich

1 sandwich.

Utensils	Ingredients
Table knife	1 or 2 slices process
Cookie sheet	American cheese
	2 slices white or dark
	rye bread
	Soft butter or margarine

1 Heat oven to 450°.

2 Place 1 or 2 slices cheese between 2 slices bread. Spread outsides of the sandwich with soft butter. Place on ungreased cookie sheet.

3 Bake in 450° oven about 12 minutes or until the cheese melts and the bread is golden brown.

Note: Instead of baking the sandwich, you can cook it in a skillet over low heat until golden brown, about 5 minutes. (Lift an edge and peek.) Turn with a pancake turner and cook about 5 minutes on the other side or until the cheese melts. Watch carefully so it doesn't burn.

Or if you have a microwave oven, you can cook the sandwich in that. Do not butter the outsides of the sandwich. Wrap it in a paper napkin and place it on a paper plate. Cook in the microwave oven about 45 seconds or until the sandwich is hot. Remove it from the oven, unwrap it and spread the outsides with soft butter or margarine.

Toasty Hot Dog Roll-Ups

8 roll-ups.

Utensils	Ingredients
Medium saucepan with cover	2 cups water
Small saucepan	8 frankfurters
Cookie sheet	½ cup butter or margarine (1 stick)
Pastry brush	8 slices white bread
Table knife	2 teaspoons prepared mustard
Tongs or fork	4 slices process American cheese
16 wooden picks	Catsup

1 Heat oven to 375°.

2 Heat 2 cups water to boiling in medium saucepan over medium heat. Carefully drop 8 frankfurters into the water. Reduce heat. Cover and simmer over low heat 5 to 8 minutes.

3 Melt ½ cup butter in small saucepan over low heat.

4 Place 8 slices bread on ungreased cookie sheet. Brush the top sides of the slices with about half of the melted butter. Spread with 2 teaspoons mustard (about ¼ teaspoon for each slice).

5 Cut 4 slices cheese diagonally in half so you have 8 cheese triangles. Top each bread slice with 1 cheese triangle.

6 Place 1 frankfurter on top of each cheese triangle with tongs.

7 Fold the bread over to make a triangle shape. Fasten with 2 wooden picks, 1 on each side, poking them through the bread and frankfurter. Brush the outside of the bread triangles with remaining melted butter.

8 Bake in 375° oven 10 to 15 minutes or until golden brown. Serve with catsup.

Note: In place of the mustard, you can spread the buttered bread with 2 teaspoons horseradish or pickle relish.

Open-Face Hamburgers

4 hamburgers.

Utensils	Ingredients
Medium bowl	½ slice white bread
Fork	½ pound ground beef
Toaster	¼ cup milk
Cookie sheet	½ teaspoon salt
Table knife	¼ teaspoon onion powder
	4 slices white bread

1 Heat oven to 400°.

2 Tear ½ slice bread into tiny pieces and place in bowl. Stir in the ground beef, ¼ cup milk, ½ teaspoon salt and ¼ teaspoon onion powder with fork.

3 Toast 4 slices bread and place on ungreased cookie sheet.

4 Spread each slice of toast with about ¼ of the ground beef mixture. Cover the edges of the toast completely to prevent them from burning—no crusts should show.

5 Bake in 400° oven about 15 minutes. (If you're not sure if the hamburgers are done, ask for another opinion.)

Pineapple-Ham Haystacks

Pictured on the back cover.

4 haystacks.

Utensils	Ingredients
Paper towels	1 can (8¼ ounces) sliced pineapple
Toaster	4 slices rye bread
Small bowl	2 tablespoons soft butter or margarine
Fork	½ teaspoon dry mustard
Table knife	4 slices cooked ham, ¼ inch thick*
Cookie sheet	4 slices process American cheese
	Paprika
	About 1 cup shoestring potatoes

1 Heat oven to 400°.

2 Drain the can of pineapple and spread the pineapple slices on paper towels to dry. Toast 4 slices bread.

3 Mix 2 tablespoons soft butter and ½ teaspoon dry mustard in bowl with fork. Spread the seasoned butter on one side of each toast slice. Place the toast buttered sides up on ungreased cookie sheet.

4 Place 1 slice ham, 1 slice cheese and 1 slice pineapple on each slice of toast, then sprinkle with paprika. Place several shoestring potatoes in the center of each pineapple slice to resemble a haystack.

5 Bake in 400° oven 10 to 12 minutes or until the cheese melts.

* You may want to trim any extra fat from the ham slices before you use them.

Shrimpy Pizzas

10 pizzas.

Utensils	Ingredients
Strainer	1 can (4½ ounces) shrimp
Cutting board	1 can (2¼ ounces) sliced ripe olives
Sharp knife	1 loaf (1 pound) Vienna bread (unsliced)
Table knife	Soft butter or margarine
Cookie sheet	2 packages (4 ounces each) shredded pizza cheese
Medium bowl	½ cup chili sauce
Spoon	2 teaspoons instant minced onion or 2 tablespoons frozen chopped onion

1 Heat oven to 375°.

2 Empty the shrimp into strainer and rinse with cold water. Drain the can of olives.

3 Cut the bread into ten 1-inch slices on cutting board.

4 Spread both sides of the bread slices with soft butter. Place on ungreased cookie sheet.

5 Mix the shrimp, olives, shredded cheese, ½ cup chili sauce and 2 teaspoons minced onion in bowl. Spread each bread slice with about 1/5 of the shrimp mixture.

6 Bake in 375° oven 5 to 10 minutes or until the cheese melts.

Note: In place of the Vienna bread, you can use 5 English muffins. Cut the muffins in half and spread only the cut sides with butter.

Beat the dough vigorously with a fork until it cleans the side of the bowl.

To knead, curve your fingers and fold the dough toward you, then push it away with the heels of your hands.

Roll each part of dough into an oval on an ungreased cookie sheet, then pinch up a rim around the edge.

Top the dough with some of the tomato sauce mixture, shredded cheese and frankfurter slices.

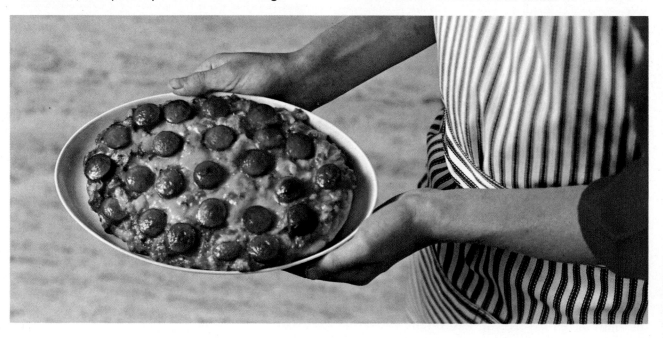

Polka Dot Pizzas

3 pizzas.

Utensils	Ingredients
Breadboard	2 cans (8 ounces each) tomato sauce
Medium bowl	3 tablespoons instant minced onion or ½ cup frozen chopped onion
2 forks	
Large bowl	
Cookie sheet	2 teaspoons oregano leaves
Rolling pin	¼ teaspoon pepper
Rubber scraper	2½ cups biscuit baking mix
Cutting board	
Sharp knife	1 package active dry yeast
	⅔ cup hot water
	2 cups shredded Cheddar or mozzarella cheese (about 8 ounces)
	6 skinless frankfurters

1 Heat oven to 425°. Rub some flour into breadboard to cover about a 10-inch area.

2 Mix the tomato sauce, 3 tablespoons minced onion, 2 teaspoons oregano and ¼ teaspoon pepper in medium bowl with fork. (You'll use this later for a topping.)

3 Mix 2½ cups baking mix and the yeast in large bowl with another fork. Stir in ⅔ cup hot water and beat vigorously until the dough cleans the side of the bowl.

4 Gently smooth the dough into a ball on the floured board. Knead 20 times. Allow the dough to rest a few minutes, then divide the dough into 3 equal parts.

5 Shape 1 part into a ball and place it in the center of ungreased cookie sheet. Rub a little flour on rolling pin and roll the ball into an oval ¼ inch thick. Pinch the edge to make a little stand-up rim.

6 Dip out ⅓ of the tomato sauce mixture (about ⅔ cup) and pour onto the oval. Spread the sauce mixture almost to the edge of the dough with rubber scraper. Sprinkle with ⅓ of the shredded cheese (about ⅔ cup).

7 Cut 2 of the frankfurters crosswise into penny slices on cutting board. Arrange the slices on the pizza.

8 Bake in 425° oven 15 to 20 minutes or until the crust is golden brown.

9 Repeat steps 5 through 8 with 2 remaining parts of dough and remaining sauce, cheese and frankfurters to make 2 more pizzas.

Note: You may want to gobble up the pizzas as they come out of the oven. If not, this is a good bake-ahead recipe. When you're ready to eat, heat the pizzas, 2 at a time, on an ungreased cookie sheet in a 300° oven about 5 minutes or until hot. The third pizza will be ready by the time you've finished eating the first 2.

Be sure to eat 4 servings of enriched or whole-grain breads and cereals every day. (You can have 1 cup cold cereal or ½ cup cooked cereal or ½ to ¾ cup cooked macaroni or rice instead of 1 slice of bread.) These foods give you quick energy and help your body do its work.

Hotsy-Totsy Doughnuts

Utensils	Ingredients
Baking pan	Sugared, glazed or plain
Aluminum foil	doughnuts (not frosted)

1 Heat oven to 325°.

2 Arrange doughnuts in a single layer in ungreased baking pan. Cover with aluminum foil.

3 Heat in 325° oven 20 minutes. Yum!

Coco-Caramel Toast

3 or 4 slices toast.

Utensils	Ingredients
Small bowl	2 tablespoons brown sugar
Spoon	2 tablespoons flaked coconut
Toaster	1 tablespoon soft butter or margarine
Table knife	3 or 4 slices white, whole wheat or raisin bread
Cookie sheet	

1 Heat oven to 325°.

2 Mix 2 tablespoons brown sugar, 2 tablespoons coconut and 1 tablespoon soft butter in bowl.

3 Toast 3 or 4 slices bread. Spread with the brown sugar mixture. Place on ungreased cookie sheet.

4 Bake in 325° oven 10 minutes.

Log Cabin Toast

1 log cabin.

Utensils	Ingredients
Custard cup	¼ cup sugar
Spoon	2 teaspoons cinnamon
Toaster	2 slices white or whole wheat bread
Table knife	
Small plate	Soft butter or margarine

1 Mix ¼ cup sugar and 2 teaspoons cinnamon in custard cup.

2 Toast 2 slices bread. Spread with soft butter. Sprinkle with the sugar-cinnamon mixture.

3 Cut each slice of toast into 4 strips. Put them together on plate like stacked logs to make the walls of a log cabin. Start from the top and eat all the logs.

Remember this whenever you use the toaster: If the toast doesn't pop up by itself, pull out the plug and get some help from someone older. *Never* try to pull out the toast with a fork or knife while the toaster is still connected—you could get a very nasty electric shock!

French Toast

6 servings.

Utensils	Ingredients
Griddle	2 eggs
Small bowl	½ cup milk
Fork	¼ teaspoon salt
Pastry brush	6 slices day-old white or
Pancake turner	raisin bread
	Powdered sugar

1 Heat griddle over medium heat or heat electric griddle to 375°.

2 Beat 2 eggs, ½ cup milk and ¼ teaspoon salt in bowl with fork until blended.

3 Grease the hot griddle with a thin layer of butter or margarine, using pastry brush.

4 Dip 6 slices bread one at a time into the egg mixture.

5 Cook the bread on the greased hot griddle until golden brown, about 4 minutes. (Lift an edge and peek.) Turn with pancake turner and cook about 4 minutes on the other side. Serve with powdered sugar.

Waffles

6 to 8 waffles.

Utensils	Ingredients
Waffle iron	2 eggs
Medium bowl	2 cups buttermilk
Egg beater	2 cups all-purpose flour*
Cup or pitcher	2 teaspoons baking
Fork	powder
	1 teaspoon baking soda
	½ teaspoon salt
	6 tablespoons shortening
	Butter or margarine
	Maple-flavored syrup

1 Heat waffle iron.

2 Beat 2 eggs in bowl until the whites and yellows are mixed. Add remaining ingredients except the butter and syrup and beat until smooth.

3 For each waffle, pour the batter from cup onto the center of the hot waffle iron. (Use about ⅔ cup batter in a 7-inch round waffle iron or about 1⅓ cups batter in a 9-inch square waffle iron.)

4 Cook about 5 minutes or until steaming stops. Remove the waffle carefully with fork. Serve with butter and syrup.

* If using self-rising flour, omit the baking powder and salt.

VARIATION

Blueberry Waffles: Follow recipe for waffles except—sprinkle 2 tablespoons blueberries over the batter for each waffle as soon as it's been poured onto the waffle iron.

Banana Pancakes

About 18 pancakes.

Utensils	Ingredients
Griddle	2 medium ripe bananas
Pastry brush	2 cups biscuit baking
Small bowl	mix
Fork	1 egg
Medium bowl	1⅓ cups milk
Egg beater	2 tablespoons sugar
Rubber scraper	Honey or currant jelly
Pancake turner	

1 Heat griddle over medium heat or heat electric griddle to 375°. Grease the hot griddle with shortening if necessary, using pastry brush.

2 Mash enough of 2 bananas in small bowl to measure 1 cup.

3 Prepare Pancakes as directed on baking mix package except—after mixing, fold the 1 cup mashed bananas and 2 tablespoons sugar into the batter with rubber scraper.

4 Continue as directed on the package. Serve with honey.

The griddle is hot enough for pancakes when you shake a few drops of water onto it and they skitter around. Some griddles don't have to be greased—to find out whether yours does or doesn't, read the manufacturer's directions.

If you like thinner pancakes, stir a little more milk into the batter; if you like thicker pancakes, stir in a little more biscuit baking mix or flour—whichever you're using.

Dit Dit Dot Pancakes

About 18 pancakes.

Utensils	Ingredients
Griddle	1 package (8 ounces)
Cutting board	fully cooked brown
Sharp knife	and serve link
Small skillet	sausages
Long-handled spoon	2 cups biscuit baking
Pastry brush	mix
Medium bowl	1 egg
Egg beater	1⅓ cups milk
Pancake turner	Grape jelly

1 Heat griddle over medium heat or heat electric griddle to 375°.

2 Cut the sausages into thin slices on cutting board. Place in skillet and heat over medium heat until brown, stirring occasionally.

3 Grease the hot griddle with shortening if necessary, using pastry brush.

4 Prepare Pancakes as directed on baking mix package except—during cooking, press the sausage slices onto the batter on the griddle.

5 Continue as directed on the package. Serve with grape jelly.

Note: You can make your own jelly for pancakes and sandwiches (see page 49).

Apple-Sausage Pancakes

Pictured on page 76.

About 18 pancakes.

Utensils	Ingredients
Griddle	2 packages (8 ounces each) fully cooked brown and serve link sausages
Large skillet	
Small saucepan	
Pastry brush	
Medium bowl	1 can (21 ounces) apple pie filling
Egg beater	
Pancake turner	2 cups biscuit baking mix
Table knife	
Serving plate	1 egg
Spoon	1⅓ to 1½ cups milk
	Butter or margarine

1 Heat griddle over medium heat or heat electric griddle to 375°.

2 Heat the sausages in skillet as directed on package. Heat the pie filling in saucepan over low heat. Keep the sausages and pie filling warm over very low heat while you prepare pancakes.

3 Grease the hot griddle with shortening if necessary, using pastry brush.

4 Prepare Pancakes as directed for thinner pancakes on baking mix package except—after mixing, for each pancake pour ¼ cup batter in an oval shape (about 5 inches long and 3 inches wide) onto the hot griddle. Continue as directed on the package.

5 Spread each pancake with butter and wrap it around a hot sausage. Place folded side down on plate and top with a spoonful of the hot pie filling.

Round-Up Pancakes

Pictured on page 76.

About 18 pancakes.

Utensils	Ingredients
Griddle	2 cups biscuit baking mix
Pastry brush	
Medium bowl	1 egg
Egg beater	1⅓ cups milk
Teaspoon	Your favorite syrup
Pancake turner	

1 Heat griddle over medium heat or heat electric griddle to 375°. Grease the hot griddle with shortening if necessary, using pastry brush.

2 Prepare Pancakes as directed on baking mix package except—after mixing, drizzle some batter from teaspoon onto the hot griddle to form an initial. (Initials must be made backward to make them appear right when the pancakes are served.)

3 When the bottom side of the initial has browned, pour about ¼ cup batter over the initial.

4 Continue as directed on the package. Serve with syrup.

Indian Maize Pancakes

Pictured on the facing page.

About 16 pancakes.

Utensils	Ingredients
Griddle	1 can (7 ounces) whole
Cup	kernel corn
Spoon	1 egg
Medium bowl	1¼ cups all-purpose
Egg beater	flour*
Pastry brush	2 tablespoons shortening
Pancake turner	1 teaspoon sugar
	1 teaspoon baking
	powder
	½ teaspoon baking soda
	½ teaspoon salt
	1¼ to 1½ cups butter-
	milk
	Homemade Pancake
	Syrup (right)

1 Heat griddle over medium heat or heat electric griddle to 375°.

2 Drain the liquid from the can of corn into cup. Spoon out ½ cup corn from the can and set aside. Pour the liquid in the cup back into the can and save the corn for another time.

3 Beat 1 egg in bowl until the white and yellow are mixed.

4 Add 1¼ cups flour, 2 tablespoons shortening, 1 teaspoon sugar, 1 teaspoon baking powder, ½ teaspoon baking soda and ½ teaspoon salt. Gradually add 1¼ to 1½ cups buttermilk.** Beat until smooth. Stir in the ½ cup corn.

5 Grease the hot griddle with shortening if necessary, using pastry brush. For each pancake, pour ¼ cup batter in a pool onto the hot griddle.

6 Cook until bubbles appear. Turn with pancake turner and cook until golden brown on the other side. (Lift an edge and peek.) Serve with Homemade Pancake Syrup.

* If using self-rising flour, omit the baking powder, baking soda and salt.

** If you like thick pancakes, use 1¼ cups; if you like thinner pancakes, use 1½ cups.

Homemade Pancake Syrup

1¾ cups syrup.

Utensils	Ingredients
Small saucepan	1½ cups brown sugar
Long-handled spoon	(packed)
	¾ cup water
	1 tablespoon butter or
	margarine
	Dash of salt
	½ teaspoon maple
	flavoring

1 Mix 1½ cups brown sugar, ¾ cup water, 1 tablespoon butter and dash of salt in saucepan.

2 Heat to boiling over medium heat, stirring constantly. Remove from heat. Stir in ½ teaspoon maple flavoring. Serve warm.

Butter Dips

18 dips.

Utensils	Ingredients
Breadboard and pastry cloth	¼ cup butter or margarine (½ stick)
Rolling pin and stockinet cover	1¼ cups all-purpose flour*
Custard cup	⅔ cup milk
Square baking pan, 9 × 9 × 2 inches	2 teaspoons sugar
Medium bowl	2 teaspoons baking powder
Fork	1 teaspoon salt
Sharp knife	

1   Heat oven to 450°. Cover breadboard with pastry cloth, tucking ends underneath. Cover rolling pin with stockinet cover. For convenience, place some flour in custard cup. Sprinkle the covered board and rolling pin lightly with the flour and rub it in until it disappears.

2   Melt ¼ cup butter in baking pan in oven. Mix 1¼ cups flour, ⅔ cup milk, 2 teaspoons sugar, 2 teaspoons baking powder and 1 teaspoon salt to a soft dough in bowl with fork.

3   Gently smooth the dough into a ball on the covered board. Knead 10 times. Roll the dough into an 8-inch square. Cut the square in half, then cut each half crosswise into 9 strips. (Dip the knife in flour to keep the dough from sticking.)

4   Dip each strip into the melted butter, turning to coat completely. Arrange the strips close together in 2 rows in the pan. Bake 15 to 20 minutes or until golden brown.

* If using self-rising flour, omit the baking powder and salt.

Apple-Cinnamon Coffee Cake

Utensils	Ingredients
Square baking pan, 9 × 9 × 2 inches	1 package (14 ounces) apple cinnamon muffin mix
Medium bowl	1 egg
Fork	½ cup milk
Wooden pick	Streusel Topping (below)

1   Heat oven to 400°. Grease baking pan with shortening.

2   Prepare the muffin mix as directed on package except—after mixing, pour the batter into the greased pan. Sprinkle with Streusel Topping.

3   Bake in 400° oven 20 to 25 minutes or until wooden pick inserted in the center comes out clean. Serve warm.

Streusel Topping

Utensils	Ingredients
Small bowl	½ cup brown sugar (packed)
Fork	⅓ cup all-purpose flour
	¼ cup butter or margarine (½ stick)
	½ teaspoon cinnamon

Mix ½ cup brown sugar, ⅓ cup flour, ¼ cup butter and ½ teaspoon cinnamon in small bowl with fork until crumbly. Now continue with Step 2.

Surprise Muffins

18 muffins.

Utensils	Ingredients
2 or 3 muffin pans	1 egg
18 paper baking cups (if you like)	1 cup milk
	¼ cup salad oil
Medium bowl	2 cups all-purpose flour*
Fork	¼ cup sugar
Small bowl	3 teaspoons baking powder
Large spoon	
Teaspoon	1 teaspoon salt
Spatula	About 3 tablespoons jelly

1 Heat oven to 400°. Grease the bottoms of 18 muffin cups with shortening or line with baking cups.

2 Beat 1 egg, 1 cup milk and ¼ cup oil in medium bowl with fork until blended.

3 Mix 2 cups flour, ¼ cup sugar, 3 teaspoons baking powder and 1 teaspoon salt in small bowl. Add all at once to the egg mixture. Stir just until the flour is moistened—the batter will look lumpy.

4 Spoon the batter into the muffin cups, filling each cup ⅓ full. Drop ½ teaspoon jelly onto the center of each and top with enough batter to fill ⅔ full. Wipe off any batter spilled on the pans.

5 Bake in 400° oven 20 to 25 minutes or until golden brown. Loosen the muffins with spatula and remove them at once or tip them on their sides in the pans to prevent them from steaming and getting soggy.

* If using self-rising flour, omit the baking powder and salt.

Birdseed Bread

Utensils	Ingredients
Medium bowl	2 cups biscuit baking mix
Fork	½ cup cold water
Cookie sheet	¼ teaspoon garlic powder
Small saucepan	
Pastry brush	¼ cup butter or margarine (½ stick)
Rubber scraper	
Table knife	2 tablespoons sesame seeds
	2 tablespoons salted sunflower nuts or chopped nuts

1 Heat oven to 425°. Mix 2 cups baking mix, ½ cup cold water and ¼ teaspoon garlic powder to a soft dough in bowl with fork.

2 Pat the dough on ungreased cookie sheet into a 10-inch circle.

3 Melt ¼ cup butter in saucepan over low heat. Remove from heat. Brush the dough circle with the melted butter. Sprinkle with 2 tablespoons sesame seeds and 2 tablespoons sunflower nuts. Firmly press the seeds and nuts into the dough with rubber scraper.

4 Cut the circle into 12 equal wedges (like a pie).

5 Bake in 425° oven 15 to 20 minutes or until golden brown. Serve warm. (The bread will break into wedges.)

Cheesy Pretzels

16 pretzels.

Utensils	Ingredients
Cookie sheet	1½ cups all-purpose
Breadboard and	flour*
pastry cloth	⅔ cup milk
Rolling pin and	½ cup shredded Cheddar
stockinet cover	cheese (about 2
Custard cup	ounces)
Medium bowl	2 tablespoons butter or
Fork	margarine, softened
Table knife	2 teaspoons baking
Small bowl	powder
Pastry brush	1 teaspoon sugar
Pancake turner	1 teaspoon salt
Wire cooling rack	1 egg
	Coarse salt

1 Heat oven to 400°. Grease cookie sheet with shortening.

2 Cover breadboard with pastry cloth, tucking ends underneath. Cover rolling pin with stockinet cover. For convenience, place some flour in custard cup. Sprinkle the covered board and rolling pin lightly with the flour and rub it in until it disappears.

3 Mix 1½ cups flour, ⅔ cups milk, ½ cup shredded cheese, 2 tablespoons butter, 2 teaspoons baking powder, 1 teaspoon sugar, and 1 teaspoon salt to a soft dough in medium bowl with fork.

4 Gently smooth the dough into a ball on the covered board. Knead 10 times. Divide the dough in half.

5 Roll one half of the dough into a rectangle, 12 inches long and 8 inches wide. Mark and cut the rectangle lengthwise into eight 1-inch strips. Make each strip narrower by folding it lengthwise in half. Pinch the edges to seal.

6 Twist each strip into a pretzel shape and place seam side down on the greased cookie sheet.

7 Beat 1 egg in small bowl with the fork until the white and yellow are mixed.

8 Brush the pretzels with the beaten egg, then sprinkle lightly with coarse salt.

9 Bake in 400° oven 20 to 25 minutes or until golden brown. Lift with pancake turner to rack.

10 Repeat steps 5 through 10 with remaining half of the dough.

* If using self-rising flour, omit the baking powder and salt.

Note: In place of the coarse salt, you can use onion salt or garlic salt or grated American cheese food.

VARIATION

Peanutty Pretzels: Follow recipe for Cheesy Pretzels except—in place of the butter, use 2 tablespoons crunchy peanut butter. Omit the shredded cheese. In place of the coarse salt, use 2 tablespoons chopped salted peanuts.

A pastry cloth to cover your breadboard and a stockinet for your rolling pin are inexpensive and handy to have. The flour you rub into the cloth keeps dough or pastry from sticking when you roll it out. The extra flour doesn't get rolled into the dough or pastry either, so whatever you bake will be tender and delicious.

Roll half of the dough into a rectangle, 12 by 8 inches, then mark it and cut it into eight 1-inch strips.

Fold each strip lengthwise in half to make it narrower. Pinch the edges together tightly to seal it.

Twist each strip to make a pretzel shape, then put the pretzels seam sides down on a greased cookie sheet.

Brush the pretzels with beaten egg, then sprinkle them with a little coarse salt.

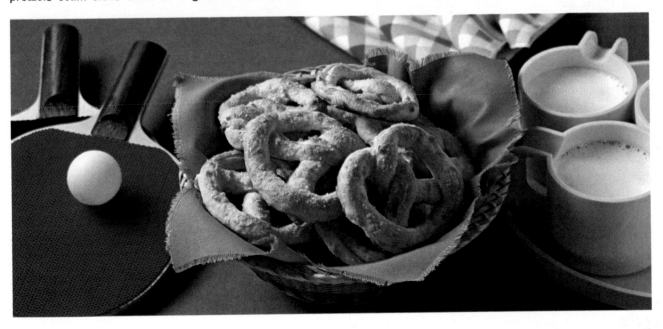

Wheaten Loaf

Utensils	Ingredients
Loaf pan, 8½ × 4½ × 2½ or 9 × 5 × 3 inches	1 package active dry yeast
Pastry brush	1¼ cups warm water (105 to 115°)
Large mixer bowl	2 tablespoons honey, brown sugar or light molasses
Long-handled spoon	
Electric mixer	2 tablespoons shortening
Rubber scraper	2 teaspoons salt
Wire cooling rack	1 cup whole wheat flour
	2 cups all-purpose flour*
	Soft butter or margarine

1 Generously grease loaf pan with shortening, using pastry brush.

2 Dissolve the yeast in 1¼ cups warm water in mixer bowl. Stir in 2 tablespoons honey, 2 tablespoons shortening, 2 teaspoons salt, 1 cup whole wheat flour and ½ cup of the all-purpose flour. Beat on medium speed until smooth, about 2 minutes. Turn off the mixer occasionally and scrape the side of the bowl. Stir in remaining flour and mix until smooth, about 1½ minutes.

3 Cover and let rise in a warm place (85°) about 30 minutes or until an impression remains when the batter is touched lightly.

4 Stir down the batter by beating with the rubber scraper about 25 strokes.

5 Spread the batter in the greased pan. Rub some flour on your hands and pat the loaf gently to smooth the top. (The batter will be sticky.)

6 Let rise until the batter is ¼ inch from the top of the 8½-inch pan or 1 inch from the top of the 9-inch pan, about 40 minutes.

7 Ten minutes before baking the bread, heat oven to 375°.

8 Bake in 375° oven 45 to 50 minutes or until the loaf is brown and sounds hollow when tapped on top. Immediately remove the loaf from the pan and place on rack.

9 Brush the top of the loaf with soft butter. Cool thoroughly before slicing.

* If using self-rising flour, omit the salt.

Cook's Corner

To make a warming tent for the Wheaten Loaf yeast batter (or other bread dough) to rise in, fill a large bowl ⅔ full of hot water. Cover it with a wire cooling rack and place the bowl of batter on the rack. Completely cover the 2 bowls and the rack with a kitchen towel. Let the batter rise as directed in Step 3 of the recipe. After your unbaked loaf is in the pan, pour fresh hot water into the large bowl. Add the rack, the loaf pan and the towel and let rise as directed in Step 6.

Frozen Dough Fun

Pictured on page 65.

1 large or 2 medium or 6 small figures.

Utensils	Ingredients
Cookie sheet	1 loaf (about 16 ounces)
Breadboard and pastry	frozen bread dough
cloth	1 egg
Rolling pin and	¼ cup milk or water
stockinet cover	Honey Dip (right)
3 custard cups	
White paper	
Pencil	
Kitchen scissors	
Fork	
Pancake turner	
Pastry brush	

1 Thaw the frozen dough (wrapped) in refrigerator overnight or at room temperature no longer than 6 hours. If more than 1 loaf comes in package, take out 1 loaf and wrap it loosely to thaw. Return remaining frozen dough in package to freezer.

2 When the dough has thawed, heat oven to 350°. Grease cookie sheet with shortening.

3 Cover breadboard with pastry cloth, tucking ends underneath. Cover rolling pin with stockinet cover. For convenience, place some flour in a custard cup. Sprinkle the covered board and rolling pin lightly with the flour and rub it in until it disappears.

4 Draw and cut out one or more patterns about 9 inches long and 7 inches wide.

5 Beat 1 egg with fork in another custard cup until the white and yellow are mixed. (You'll use this later for a glaze.) Pour ¼ cup milk into another custard cup. (You'll use this later for a kind of glue.)

6 Roll the thawed dough into a rectangle about 9 inches long, 7 inches wide and ¼ to ½ inch thick on the covered board.

7 Spread 1 or 2 drops of the milk on the back of the pattern, then place the pattern wet side down on top of the dough. Cut around the pattern with the scissors.

8 Lift the cut-out dough with pancake turner to the greased cookie sheet. Gently peel off the pattern. Pat down or reshape the dough as you like. Cut out pieces from the dough scraps to use for eyes, hair, feet or decorations. Dip the pieces in the milk to make them stick, then attach them.

9 Brush the dough figure with the beaten egg. Bake in 350° oven 25 minutes or until golden brown.

10 Is your dough figure too beautiful to eat? If you do decide to eat it, stir up some Honey Dip, break off chunks of bread and dip them in the dip.

Note: To make markings such as owl's feathers, make snips in the dough with scissors before baking. To add teeth to animals such as an alligator, stick miniature marshmallows to its open mouth with dabs of canned frosting after the figure is baked and cooled.

Honey Dip

Utensils	Ingredients
Small bowl	¼ cup butter or
Fork	margarine, softened
	¼ cup honey
	Nutmeg

Beat ¼ cup butter and ¼ cup honey with fork in bowl. Sprinkle with a little nutmeg.

Stretchy French Loaf

Utensils
Cookie sheet
Kitchen scissors
Pastry brush

Ingredients
1 loaf (about 1 pound)
   frozen white bread
   dough
2 teaspoons poppy
   seeds

1 Thaw the frozen dough (wrapped) in refrigerator overnight or at room temperature no longer than 6 hours. If more than 1 loaf comes in package, take out 1 loaf and wrap it loosely to thaw. Return remaining frozen dough in package to freezer.

2 Grease cookie sheet with shortening. Place the thawed dough diagonally on the greased cookie sheet. Roll the dough with your hands to stretch it almost to the edges of the cookie sheet.

3 Cut 3 or 4 diagonal slashes in the top of the dough with scissors. Brush the dough with water and sprinkle with 2 teaspoons poppy seeds.

4 Let rise in a warm place (85°) 25 to 30 minutes or until an impression remains when the dough is touched lightly.

5 Ten minutes before baking the bread, heat oven to 350°.

6 Bake in 350° oven about 30 minutes or until golden brown.

Cheesy Slices

About 20 slices.

Utensils
Cutting board
Sharp knife
Cookie sheet
Small saucepan
Long-handled spoon
Pastry brush

Ingredients
1 loaf (1 pound) French
   bread
½ cup butter or mar-
   garine (1 stick)
¼ teaspoon garlic salt
Grated American cheese
   food or grated
   Parmesan cheese

1 Heat oven to 450°.

2 Cut the bread into 1-inch slices on cutting board. Place the slices on ungreased cookie sheet.

3 Melt ½ cup butter in saucepan over low heat. Remove from heat. Stir in ¼ teaspoon garlic salt.

4 Brush the slices with the seasoned butter and sprinkle with grated cheese.

5 Bake in 450° oven 3 to 5 minutes or until hot.

Note: Instead of melting butter or margarine, you can soften them in the microwave oven. *Butter:* Place a stick of cold butter on a plate. Place in the oven. Cook 15 seconds. Let stand 10 seconds. If necessary, cook 5 seconds longer. *Margarine:* Place a stick of cold margarine on a plate. Place in oven. Cook 5 seconds.

Pictured: Tacos Sealed with Refried Beans (page 92)

Mmm – Main Dishes

Oven Cobblestone Stew

6 to 8 servings.

Utensils	Ingredients
Cutting board	2 pounds beef round
Sharp knife	steak or stew meat
Vegetable parer	6 medium carrots
Oblong baking pan,	6 medium potatoes
13 × 9 × 2 inches	6 small onions
Fork	1 can (10¾ ounces)
Small bowl	condensed cream of
Spoon	mushroom soup
Aluminum foil	1 envelope (about 1
2 teaspoons	ounce) brown gravy
	mix
	¼ cup water
	1 teaspoon horseradish
	½ teaspoon salt
	Cobblestone Biscuits
	(right)

1 Heat oven to 325°.

2 Cut the meat into 1-inch cubes on cutting board. Wash and pare 6 carrots and 6 potatoes and peel 6 onions. Cut each of the carrots and potatoes in half.

3 Mix the meat and vegetables in ungreased baking pan with fork and spread to the edges of the pan.

4 Pour the soup into bowl. Stir in remaining ingredients except Cobblestone Biscuits and pour over the meat and vegetables in the pan. Cover tightly with aluminum foil.

5 Bake in 325° oven 3 hours.

6 While the stew is baking, mix the dough for Cobblestone Biscuits and refrigerate it.

7 Carefully remove the stew from oven. Increase oven temperature to 450°.

8 Drop teaspoonfuls of the biscuit dough about ½ inch apart onto the stew. (Use 2 teaspoons, one to push the dough from the other. Work as fast as you can.)

9 Bake about 10 minutes or until the biscuits are golden brown.

Cobblestone Biscuits

Utensils	Ingredients
Medium bowl	1 cup biscuit baking
Fork	mix
	½ cup grated American
	cheese food
	¼ cup cold water
	2 tablespoons mayon-
	naise or salad
	dressing

Mix all ingredients to a soft dough in bowl with fork. Now continue with Step 6.

Growing boys and girls need 2 or more servings of meat every day. (You can substitute fish, poultry, cheese or eggs for a serving of meat if you like.) These protein-rich foods help make muscles and help you grow and stay strong.

Chicken-Fried Cubed Steaks

4 servings.

Utensils	Ingredients
Large skillet	2 tablespoons shortening
Tongs	1 package (2⅜ ounces)
Pancake turner	seasoned coating mix
Serving platter	for chicken (with
Fork	shaker bag)
	4 beef cubed steaks
	(1½ to 2 pounds)
	¼ to ⅓ cup warm water

1 Melt 2 tablespoons shortening in skillet over low heat. While the shortening melts, measure 4 tablespoons of the coating mix into the shaker bag. (Rewrap remaining coating mix to use another time.) Shake 4 cubed steaks, one at a time, in the shaker bag until coated. (You'll use remaining coating mix in the shaker bag later.)

2 Place the coated steaks in the hot skillet with tongs. Increase heat to medium-high and fry the steaks about 5 minutes on each side. (You may want to ask for a second opinion in deciding when they are cooked through.)

3 Lift the steaks to platter with pancake turner. Shake the coating mix remaining in the shaker bag into the skillet. Add ¼ to ⅓ cup warm water and stir with fork to mix with the coating mix and meat scrapings. Heat to boiling. Stir the sauce and pour over the steaks.

Hamburger Fake Cake

4 servings.

Utensils	Ingredients
Large bowl	1½ pounds ground beef
2 forks	¼ cup frozen chopped
8-inch pie pan	onion
Medium saucepan	¼ cup water
Pancake turner	1 teaspoon salt
Serving platter	1 teaspoon soy sauce
Spatula	¼ teaspoon pepper
	Instant mashed potato
	puffs (enough for
	4 servings)
	1⅓ cups water
	⅓ cup milk
	2 tablespoons butter
	½ teaspoon salt
	Catsup and prepared
	mustard (in squirt
	bottles if possible)

1 Heat oven to 350°. Mix the ground beef, ¼ cup chopped onion, ¼ cup water, 1 teaspoon salt, 1 teaspoon soy sauce and ¼ teaspoon pepper in bowl with fork.

2 Place the ground beef mixture in ungreased pie pan and shape into a round mound (like a cake). Bake in 350° oven 45 minutes.

3 Five minutes before the hamburger is done, prepare the mashed potato puffs for 4 servings in saucepan with fork as directed on package.

4 Remove the hamburger from the oven. Lift to platter with pancake turner. Frost with the mashed potatoes, using spatula.

5 Decorate the top of the frosted hamburger cake with the catsup and mustard.

Juicy Hamburgers

6 hamburgers.

Utensils	Ingredients
Medium bowl	1½ pounds ground beef
Fork	¼ cup water
Large skillet or baking pan with rack	3 to 4 teaspoons instant minced onion* or ¼ cup frozen chopped onion
	1 teaspoon salt
	1 teaspoon Worcestershire sauce
	¼ teaspoon pepper

1 Mix all ingredients in bowl with fork.

2 Shape the mixture with your hands into 6 patties about ¾ inch thick.

3 Cook in one of the following ways:

To panfry: Fry the patties in skillet over medium heat 5 minutes on each side. (Ask someone to help you decide when the patties are done if you're not sure.)

To oven-bake: Heat oven to 350°. Place the patties on rack in baking pan. Bake in 350° oven 20 minutes. (Ask someone to help you decide when the patties are done if you're not sure.)

*Before adding instant minced onion, soak in an equal amount of water 3 to 4 minutes.

Sloppy Joes

6 to 8 sandwiches.

Utensils	Ingredients
Cutting board	1 celery stalk
Sharp knife	1 pound ground beef
Large skillet	3 tablespoons instant minced onion
Long-handled spoon	1 teaspoon salt
Cookie sheet	⅛ teaspoon pepper
Pancake turner	1 jar (about 16 ounces) spaghetti sauce
Serving platter	6 to 8 hamburger buns

1 Wash 1 celery stalk and pinch off leaves. Chop the celery into ½-inch pieces on cutting board.

2 Crumble the ground beef into skillet. Cook and stir over medium-high heat until brown on all sides, about 10 minutes. Spoon out any fat and throw it away.

3 Stir the celery, 3 tablespoons minced onion, 1 teaspoon salt, ⅛ teaspoon pepper and the spaghetti sauce into the ground beef. Heat to boiling, stirring constantly. Reduce heat. Simmer uncovered over low heat 10 minutes, stirring occasionally.

4 Cut 6 to 8 hamburger buns crosswise in half and place cut sides up on ungreased cookie sheet. Adjust broiler rack so the tops of the buns will be 4 to 5 inches from heat. Set oven control at broil and/or 550°.

5 Toast the buns until light brown. Watch carefully—it will take just 1 or 2 minutes. Lift the buns to platter with pancake turner. Spoon the ground beef mixture onto bottom half of each bun and cover with top half.

Bumpy Meatballs

4 servings.

Utensils	Ingredients
Medium bowl	1½ pounds ground beef
Fork	½ cup uncooked regular
Large skillet	rice
Slotted spoon	¼ cup water
1½-quart casserole	1 tablespoon instant
with cover	minced onion*
Small bowl	1 teaspoon salt
Spoon	1 teaspoon Worcester-
	shire sauce
	¼ teaspoon pepper
	1 can (11 ounces)
	condensed Cheddar
	cheese soup
	¼ cup milk
	Paprika

1 Heat oven to 350°.

2 Mix all ingredients except the soup, milk and paprika in medium bowl with fork. Shape the mixture with your hands into 20 meatballs about the size of golf balls.

3 Brown several meatballs at a time in skillet over medium-high heat. As the meatballs brown, lift them with slotted spoon to ungreased casserole and add more meatballs to the skillet.

4 Mix the soup and ¼ cup milk in small bowl until smooth. Pour over the browned meatballs in the casserole. Sprinkle with paprika.

5 Bake in 350° oven 1 hour to 1 hour and 15 minutes or until the rice is tender.

* Before adding instant minced onion, soak in an equal amount of water 3 to 4 minutes.

One-Pot Italian Spaghetti

4 to 6 servings.

Utensils	Ingredients
Dutch oven with	1 pound ground beef
cover	2 tablespoons instant
Long-handled spoon	minced onion or
	⅓ cup frozen chopped
	onion
	1 can (8 ounces) tomato
	sauce
	1 can (15 ounces)
	spaghetti sauce with
	mushrooms
	1½ teaspoons salt
	1 teaspoon sugar
	2 cups water
	1 package (about 7
	ounces) long spaghetti
	3 tablespoons grated
	Parmesan cheese
	(if you like)

1 Crumble the ground beef into Dutch oven. Cook and stir over medium-high heat until brown on all sides, about 10 minutes. Spoon out any fat and throw it away.

2 Stir 2 tablespoons minced onion, the tomato sauce and spaghetti sauce into the ground beef. Add 1½ teaspoons salt, 1 teaspoon sugar, 2 cups water and the spaghetti (uncooked). Heat to boiling over medium-high heat, stirring occasionally to prevent sticking.

3 Reduce heat. Cover and simmer over low heat about 15 minutes or until the spaghetti is tender. Remove from heat and stir once. Sprinkle with 3 tablespoons grated cheese just before serving.

No-Crust Wide-Eyed Pizzas

4 pizzas.

Utensils	Ingredients
Medium bowl	1 can (8 ounces) tomato sauce
Fork	1 pound ground beef
Jelly roll pan, 15½ × 10½ × 1 inch	½ cup packaged dry bread crumbs
Rubber scraper	½ teaspoon salt
Cutting board	½ teaspoon oregano
Sharp knife	2 pimiento-stuffed or pitted black olives
	½ cup shredded mozzarella cheese (about 2 ounces)
	½ cup shredded Cheddar cheese (about 2 ounces)
	4 slices canned pimiento

1 Heat oven to 425°.

2 Measure out ½ cup of the tomato sauce. (You'll also use the sauce remaining in the can, so keep it handy.)

3 Mix the ground beef, ½ cup bread crumbs, the ½ cup tomato sauce, ½ teaspoon salt and ½ teaspoon oregano in bowl with fork.

4 Divide the ground beef mixture into 4 equal parts. Place the parts several inches apart in ungreased jelly roll pan. Pat each into a 4½-inch circle about ½ inch thick. Pinch the edge of each circle to make a little stand-up rim.

5 Pour about 2 tablespoons of the remaining tomato sauce into the center of each circle and spread it to the edge with rubber scraper.

6 Bake in 425° oven 15 to 20 minutes. (Ask someone else to help you decide when the pizzas are done if you're not sure.)

7 While the pizzas are baking, cut 2 olives crosswise into 4 slices each on cutting board.

8 Remove the pan from oven and turn off oven. Sprinkle each pizza with about 2 tablespoons shredded mozzarella cheese for a face and about 2 tablespoons shredded Cheddar cheese around the edge for hair. Use the olive and pimiento slices to make the eyes and mouth. Return the pizzas to warm oven and heat about 5 minutes or until the cheese melts.

Cook's Corner

What you eat makes you what you are. Most foods contain many hidden helpers called nutrients—magical substances that keep you healthy, help you grow and keep your body in good repair. To stay full of pep, try at least a little of every kind of food served at your table. A good variety of meats, fruits and vegetables, dairy foods and cereal foods will give a shine to your hair, a sparkle to your smile and a bounce to your step.

Tacos Sealed
with Refried Beans

Pictured on page 85.

10 tacos.

Utensils	Ingredients
Cutting board	Lettuce wedge (about
Sharp knife	1 inch thick)
3 small serving bowls	1 large tomato
Large skillet	1 package (4 ounces)
Long-handled spoon	shredded Cheddar
Cookie sheet	cheese (about 1 cup)
Pancake turner	1 pound ground beef
Serving platter	3 tablespoons instant
Large serving bowl	minced onion or
	½ cup frozen chopped
	onion
	1 can (15 ounces)
	tomato sauce
	1 teaspoon garlic salt
	1 teaspoon chili powder
	Dash of pepper
	Refried Beans (below)
	1 package (5 ounces)
	taco shells (10 shells)
	Bottled taco sauce

1 Chop the lettuce into long shreds on cutting board. Place the lettuce in small serving bowl.

2 Wash and cut stem end from 1 tomato. Chop into ¼-inch pieces. Place in another small serving bowl. Empty the shredded cheese into another small serving bowl.

3 Heat oven to temperature given on taco shell package.

4 Crumble the ground beef into skillet. Cook and stir over medium-high heat until brown on all sides, about 10 minutes. Spoon out any fat and throw it away.

5 Stir 3 tablespoons minced onion, the tomato sauce, 1 teaspoon garlic salt, 1 teaspoon chili powder and dash of pepper into the ground beef. Reduce heat. Simmer uncovered over low heat 15 minutes, stirring occasionally.

6 While the ground beef mixture is simmering, prepare Refried Beans and heat the taco shells as directed on package. Lift the taco shells to platter with pancake turner.

7 Pour the ground beef mixture into large serving bowl. Serve along with the tacos, lettuce, tomato and cheese. Let each person make his or her own taco combination, sealing the taco by spreading the opening with the Refried Beans. Pass taco sauce.

Refried Beans

Utensils	Ingredients
Large saucepan	2 cans (about 16
Long-handled spoon	ounces each) hot
Small serving bowl	chili beans or baked
	beans
	¼ teaspoon chili powder
	¼ teaspoon onion salt
	Dash of garlic salt

Drain liquid from the cans of chili beans into saucepan. Stir in ¼ teaspoon chili powder, ¼ teaspoon onion salt and dash of garlic salt. Cook over low heat 5 minutes. Stir in the beans. Increase heat to medium and cook until the beans are dry, about 20 minutes, stirring frequently. Pour into serving bowl. Now continue with Step 6.

Basic Meat Loaf

8 to 10 servings.

Utensils	Ingredients
Large bowl	1 egg
Large fork	½ cup milk
Table knife	¾ cup quick-cooking
Oblong baking pan,	oats
13 × 9 × 2 inches	3 teaspoons salt
	1 teaspoon instant beef
	bouillon
	3 tablespoons instant
	minced onion* or
	½ cup frozen chopped
	onion
	2 teaspoons horseradish
	2½ pounds lean ground
	beef

1   Heat oven to 350°.

2   Mix all ingredients in bowl with fork. (This will take some mixing! Cutting through several times with knife will help.)

3   Place the ground beef mixture in ungreased baking pan. Shape with your hands into a loaf about 9 inches long, 5 inches wide and 3 inches thick.

4   Bake in 350° oven uncovered 1 hour and 30 minutes or until crusty and brown.

* Before adding instant minced onion, soak in an equal amount of water 3 to 4 minutes.

VARIATIONS

Zingy Horseradish Meat Loaf: Follow recipe for Basic Meat Loaf except—before baking, spread ¼ cup horseradish over the top of the loaf.

Barbecue Meat Loaf: Follow recipe for Basic Meat Loaf except—before baking, spread ¼ cup barbecue sauce over the top of the loaf.

Cheesy Meat Loaf: Follow recipe for Basic Meat Loaf except—after baking, overlap three 4-inch-square cheese slices on the top of the loaf. The heat from the loaf will melt the cheese.

Flowerpot Meat Loaf: Follow recipe for Basic Meat Loaf except—after baking, make a flower design, using a ring of sliced pimiento-stuffed olives for the flower petals; a cherry tomato for the center of the flower; green pepper strips for the stem, leaves and flowerpot and celery leaves for grass.

Football Meat Loaf: Follow recipe for Basic Meat Loaf except—before baking, shape the meat mixture into an oval that looks like a football, about 8 inches long and 5 inches wide at the middle. After baking, arrange strips of canned sliced pimiento (drained) on top to look like the lacings of a football. If you like, serve on a bed of spinach: Cook three 10-ounce packages frozen spinach as directed on packages. Drain spinach and arrange around football. (You don't like spinach? Try it—you might be surprised!)

Meat Loaf Rings

8 rings.

Utensils	Ingredients
Waxed paper	Basic Meat Loaf
Spoon	(page 93)
Pancake turner	Cheesy Potatoes
Jelly roll pan,	or Carrot Nuggets
15½ × 10½ × 1 inch,	(right)
or 2 oblong baking	
pans, 13 × 9 × 2	
inches	
Serving platter	
Ice-cream scoop or	
large spoon	

1 Heat oven to 350°.

2 Prepare Basic Meat Loaf except—before baking, spoon half of the ground beef mixture onto waxed paper.

3 Divide this half of the mixture into 4 equal parts. Roll each part with your hands into a strip 9 inches long and 1½ inches thick. Press the ends of each strip together firmly to make a ring.

4 Lift the rings with pancake turner to ungreased jelly roll pan.

5 Divide remaining ground beef mixture into 4 equal parts and make 4 more rings. Lift them to the pan.

6 Bake uncovered in 350° oven about 30 minutes or until crusty and brown. Five minutes before the rings are done, make Cheesy Potatoes or Carrot Nuggets. Lift the rings to platter with pancake turner and fill each with a scoop (about ⅓ cup) of potatoes or a mound of carrots.

Cheesy Potatoes

Utensils	Ingredients
Large saucepan	Instant mashed potato
Fork	puffs (enough for
	8 servings)
	2⅔ cups water
	⅔ cup milk
	4 tablespoons butter or
	margarine (½ stick)
	1 teaspoon salt
	¼ cup shredded Ameri-
	can cheese

Prepare the mashed potato puffs as directed on package for 8 servings. Stir ¼ cup shredded cheese into the hot mashed potatoes.

Carrot Nuggets

Utensils	Ingredient
Medium saucepan with	1 package (10 ounces)
cover	frozen carrot nuggets
Fork	

Cook the carrots as directed on package. Now continue with Step 6.

VARIATION

Potatoes Baked in Meat Loaf Rings: Follow recipe for Meat Loaf Rings except—before baking, spoon 3 or 4 canned whole potatoes into the center of each ring. (You will need two 16-ounce cans of potatoes.) Spoon about 1 tablespoon catsup onto each mound of potatoes. Bake as directed 35 minutes.

On waxed paper, roll the meat loaf mixture into strips 9 inches long and 1½ inches thick.

Shape each strip into a ring, pressing the ends together firmly so they won't come apart in baking.

Potatoes Baked in Meat Loaf Rings, Meat Loaf Rings with Cheesy Potatoes and with Carrot Nuggets

Hamburger Dinners in Foil

4 dinners.

Utensils	Ingredients
Medium bowl	1 pound ground beef
Fork	¾ teaspoon salt
4 sheets heavy-duty	¼ teaspoon dry mustard
aluminum foil,	1 large mild onion
18 × 15 inches	2 medium potatoes
Cutting board	Salt
Sharp knife	4 tablespoons catsup
Vegetable parer	2 medium carrots
Oblong baking pan,	Pepper
13 × 9 × 2 inches	4 teaspoons butter or
	margarine

1 Heat oven to 375°.

2 Mix thoroughly the ground beef, ¾ teaspoon salt and ¼ teaspoon dry mustard in bowl with fork. Divide the ground beef mixture into 4 equal parts and place each in the center of a sheet of heavy-duty aluminum foil.

3 Shape each part with your hands into a patty about ¾ inch thick. Peel 1 onion and cut it in half. Wrap one half and refrigerate to use another time. Ask someone older to help you cut remaining half into 4 slices on cutting board—onions are very slippery! Place 1 onion slice on each patty.

4 Wash and pare 2 potatoes, then cut each crosswise in half. Allowing half of a potato for each dinner, cut the halves into ¼-inch slices and place on top of the onion slices. Sprinkle each layer of potato slices with a pinch of salt and top with 1 tablespoon catsup.

5 Wash and pare 2 carrots, then cut each crosswise in half. Allowing half of a carrot for each dinner, cut halves into ¼-inch sticks and place on top of the potato slices. Sprinkle each layer of carrots with a pinch of salt and a pinch of pepper. Top each dinner with 1 teaspoon butter.

6 Bring the long sides of the foil up to meet above the food. Press the top edges of the foil together and make a series of folds until foil is close to the food. Crease the unfolded ends to points and fold under. Place the foil packets in ungreased baking pan.

7 Bake the hamburger dinners in 375° oven 1 hour and 15 minutes.

Note: Be careful when you open the hamburger dinners—they're steaming hot!

Luncheon Meat-Biscuit Bake

4 servings.

Utensils	Ingredients
Paper towels	1 can (12 ounces) pork
Square glass baking	luncheon meat
dish, 8 × 8 × 2 inches	1 can (8¾ ounces)
Sharp knife	unpeeled apricot
Medium bowl	halves
Fork	12 whole cloves
Tablespoon	2 cups biscuit baking
Small bowl	mix
Spoon	½ cup cold water
	½ cup apricot preserves
	1 tablespoon water
	½ teaspoon dry mustard

1 Heat oven to 425°.

2 Remove the luncheon meat from the can and drain on paper towels. Place the meat in the center of ungreased baking dish. Drain the can of apricot halves.

3 Cutting a little more than halfway through, divide the luncheon meat into twelve ¼-inch slices. Poke 1 clove into the top of each slice.

4 Mix 2 cups baking mix and ½ cup cold water to a soft dough in medium bowl with fork. Drop the dough by tablespoonfuls into the baking dish, making a ring around the luncheon meat. Place the apricot halves evenly on top of the dough ring and press gently into the dough.

5 Mix ½ cup apricot preserves, 1 tablespoon water and ½ teaspoon dry mustard in small bowl. Spoon over the luncheon meat and dough.

6 Bake in 425° oven 25 to 30 minutes or until biscuits are golden brown.

Fried Ham Slice

4 or 5 servings.

Utensils	Ingredient
Cutting board	1 slice cooked smoked
Sharp knife	ham, ½ inch thick
Large skillet	
Fork	

1 Trim the fat from the ham slice on cutting board. Rub skillet with a small piece of the fat.

2 Fry the ham slice over medium heat until light brown, about 3 minutes on each side, turning with fork. Cut the ham into serving size pieces.

VARIATION

Baked Ham Slice: Follow recipe for Fried Ham Slice except—heat oven to 325°. After trimming the fat, place the ham slice in an ungreased baking dish. If you like, mix ½ cup brown sugar (packed), ¼ teaspoon dry mustard and 1½ teaspoons vinegar and spread it on the ham slice. Bake uncovered in 325° oven 30 minutes.

Ham Kabobs with Red Currant Sauce

4 kabobs.

Utensils	Ingredients
Jelly roll pan, 15½ × 10½ × 1 inch	1 can (8¼ ounces) sliced pineapple
Aluminum foil (if you like)	1 can (8 ounces) sweet potatoes in syrup
Cutting board	
Sharp knife	1¼ pounds cooked smoked ham
4 skewers, 8 inches long	1 orange
Small saucepan	4 maraschino cherries
Long-handled spoon	1 jar (10 ounces) currant jelly
Pastry brush	1 teaspoon horseradish

1 Heat oven to 400°. Line jelly roll pan with aluminum foil so the pan will be easy to clean.

2 Drain the cans of sliced pineapple and sweet potatoes.

3 Trim the fat from the ham and cut ham into 12 cubes (about 1 inch square) on cutting board.

4 Cut 1 orange crosswise in half, then cut each half into 2 wedges.

5 Place on each skewer (in any order you like) 3 ham cubes, 1 sweet potato, 1 orange wedge, 1 pineapple slice and 1 maraschino cherry. (Here's a suggestion: ham cube, sweet potato, pineapple bow (right), ham cube, orange wedge, ham cube.)

6 Mix the currant jelly and 1 teaspoon horseradish in saucepan. Heat over medium-low heat until the jelly melts. Brush all sides of the kabobs with the currant sauce. Don't use all the mixture right now. Place the skewers in the foil-lined pan.

7 Bake in 400° oven 10 minutes. Remove the pan from oven and brush the kabobs again with the currant sauce.

8 Bake 5 to 10 minutes. If you have any currant sauce left, brush the kabobs again before serving.

Note: If the sweet potatoes are too soft to stay on the skewers, heat them in a saucepan over medium heat and serve them with the kabobs.

Cook's Corner

A pineapple bow looks pretty on a kabob and tastes good too! Slip the skewer through one side of a pineapple ring, then through a maraschino cherry, then through the other side of the pineapple ring.

Shape the meat mixture into a round mound with a 1-inch-deep "crater" in the center.

Prepare the Cheese Topping and pour it into the crater (or fill it with hot dog relish instead).

Crater Ham Loaf

6 servings.

Utensils	Ingredients
Medium bowl	2 eggs
Fork	1 pound ground cooked smoked ham
Square baking pan, 9 × 9 × 2 inches	1 pound ground lean pork
	3 cups whole wheat flake cereal
	1 cup milk
	1 teaspoon salt
	⅛ teaspoon pepper
	Cheese Topping (right)

1 Heat oven to 375°.

2 Mix thoroughly all ingredients except Cheese Topping in bowl with fork until there are no streaks.

3 Place the meat mixture in ungreased baking pan. Shape with your hands into a round mound. Gently press down the center and build up the side to make a wall 1 inch high and 1 inch wide around the outside of the circle. There will be a 1-inch-deep "crater" in the center.

4 Prepare the Cheese Topping and pour it into the crater. Bake uncovered in 375° oven 1 hour or until golden brown on top.

Cheese Topping

Utensils	Ingredients
Small bowl	1 egg
Fork	2 tablespoons milk
	1 package (4 ounces) your favorite shredded cheese (about 1 cup)
	¼ teaspoon dry mustard
	¼ teaspoon Worcester-shire sauce

Beat 1 egg and 2 tablespoons milk in bowl with fork until blended. Stir in remaining ingredients. Now continue with Step 4.

Note: In place of the Cheese Topping, you can use 1 cup hot dog relish.

Sticky Barbecued Ribs

5 or 6 servings.

Utensils	Ingredients
Cutting board	1 large onion
Sharp knife	1 cup catsup
Medium saucepan	¼ cup vinegar
Long-handled spoon	3 tablespoons brown
Dutch oven with cover	sugar
Tongs	2 tablespoons flour
Waxed paper	1 teaspoon salt
Deep platter or soup	1 teaspoon paprika
tureen	½ teaspoon curry
	powder
	½ teaspoon dry mustard
	¼ teaspoon chili powder
	1 can (10½ ounces)
	condensed consommé
	(beef gelatin added)
	3 pounds spareribs

1 Peel 1 onion and ask someone older to help you slice it on cutting board. (Those onions do slip around!)

2 Empty 1 cup catsup, ¼ cup vinegar, 3 tablespoons brown sugar, 2 tablespoons flour, 1 teaspoon salt, 1 teaspoon paprika, ½ teaspoon curry powder, ½ teaspoon dry mustard and ¼ teaspoon chili powder into saucepan. Stir in the consommé and onion slices. (You'll use this as a sauce later.)

3 Cut the spareribs into 6 pieces (try to make them about the same size).

4 Arrange oven racks so Dutch oven will fit on the lower rack. Heat oven to 350°.

5 Cook 3 pieces of ribs in Dutch oven over medium-high heat, turning with tongs to brown them on all sides. As the pieces brown, lift them with the tongs to waxed paper to make room for the other pieces. Once all the pieces are brown, place them meaty sides up in the Dutch oven.

6 Pour the seasoned consommé over the ribs. (Now you see why you used a saucepan —for easier pouring.)

7 Bake the ribs uncovered in 350° oven 1 hour and 15 minutes. Cover and bake 30 minutes. Lift the ribs with the tongs onto deep platter. Stir the sauce in the Dutch oven and pour it over the ribs.

Baked Pork Tenderloins

4 to 6 servings.

Utensils	Ingredients
Shallow roasting pan	2 pork tenderloins
with rack	(¾ pound each)
Small saucepan	1 jar (12 ounces) peach
Spoon	or apricot jam
Cutting board	1 teaspoon salt
Sharp knife	1 teaspoon dry mustard
	1 teaspoon soy sauce

1 Heat oven to 350°. Place the tenderloins on rack in the roasting pan.

2 Mix remaining ingredients in saucepan. Spoon about half of the sauce over the tenderloins.

3 Bake the tenderloins in 350° oven 1 hour and 30 minutes.

4 Heat remaining sauce in the saucepan over low heat. Ask someone older to slice the tenderloins into ¼-inch diagonal slices on cutting board—it's hard to do. Serve the tenderloins with remaining sauce.

Bologna Daisies and Macaroni

4 servings.

Utensils	Ingredients
Medium saucepan with cover	6 cups water
Cutting board	¾-pound ring bologna
Sharp knife	2 teaspoons shortening
Large skillet	1 package (7.5 ounces) macaroni and cheese
Pancake turner	1 tablespoon butter or margarine
Colander	1½ cups hot water
Long-handled spoon	
Serving platter	

1 Heat 6 cups water to boiling in saucepan (to use to prepare the macaroni and cheese).

2 Peel casing off the bologna. Cut the bologna into ¼-inch slices on cutting board. Make cuts about ¼ inch deep at ½-inch intervals around the edges of the slices so they look like daisies.

3 Melt 2 teaspoons shortening in skillet over low heat. Cook the bologna slices in the shortening until they are brown on one side. Turn with pancake turner and brown them on the other side.

4 While the bologna slices are browning, prepare the macaroni and cheese as directed on package. (If the bologna slices finish browning before the macaroni and cheese is ready, keep them warm over very low heat.)

5 Serve the macaroni and cheese on platter, with the bologna daisies arranged in a ring around it.

Glazed Chicken Drumsticks

About 14 drumsticks.

Utensils	Ingredients
Paper towels	3 pounds chicken drumsticks
Oblong baking dish, 13½ × 9 × 2 inches	3 tablespoons soy sauce
Small bowl	2 tablespoons honey
Fork	1 tablespoon salad oil
Aluminum foil	1 tablespoon chili sauce
Broiler pan with rack	½ teaspoon salt
Tongs	¼ teaspoon ginger
Pastry brush	⅛ teaspoon garlic powder
Fork	

1 Wash the drumsticks and pat dry with paper towels. Place in ungreased baking dish.

2 Mix remaining ingredients in bowl with fork and pour over the drumsticks.

3 Cover the baking dish with aluminum foil and refrigerate at least 1 hour.

4 When the drumsticks have been refrigerated at least 1 hour, heat oven to 375°.

5 Lift the drumsticks with tongs onto rack in the broiler pan. Brush the drumsticks with the sauce remaining in the baking dish.

6 Bake in 375° oven 50 to 60 minutes or until the drumsticks are tender when pierced with fork.

Note: Many oven and broiler pans now have nonstick wipe-clean finishes. If your broiler pan isn't easy to clean, you may want to line it with aluminum foil.

Lift the fried bologna slices into muffin cups and press down so they fit the cups.

Carefully break an egg into the center of each bologna cup to hold it down.

Loosen the baked bologna cups with a table knife and lift them from the muffin pan with a spoon.

Eggs in Bologna Cups

6 servings.

Utensils	Ingredients
Pastry brush	2 teaspoons shortening
Muffin pan	6 slices bologna, each
Large skillet	about 4 inches across
Tongs or pancake	6 eggs
turner	6 teaspoons milk
Table knife	Salt
Spoon	Pepper
Serving platter	Paprika

1 Heat oven to 375°.

2 Grease 6 muffin cups with some shortening, using pastry brush.

3 Melt 2 teaspoons shortening in skillet over low heat.

4 Place 3 slices bologna in the skillet and fry until the edges curl and the centers puff. Lift each slice with tongs into a muffin cup and press down so the slice fits the cup. Repeat with remaining bologna slices.

5 Break 1 egg into the center of each bologna slice to hold it down.

6 Pour 1 teaspoon milk over each egg. Sprinkle eggs lightly with salt, pepper and paprika.

7 Bake uncovered in 375° oven 15 to 20 minutes or until the eggs are set.

8 Loosen each bologna cup with knife and lift to platter with spoon.

Twin Eggs in Toast Basket

4 servings.

Utensils	Ingredients
Table knife	Soft butter or margarine
4 individual baking dishes or 10-ounce custard cups	4 slices bread
	8 eggs
	4 teaspoons milk
2 forks (if you like)	Salt
Serving platter (if you like)	Pepper
	Paprika

1 Heat oven to 350°.

2 Generously spread 4 slices bread with soft butter. Press each slice buttered side down in a baking dish.

3 Break 2 eggs into each bread slice. Pour 1 teaspoon milk over the eggs in each dish and sprinkle with salt, pepper and paprika.

4 Bake in 350° oven 15 to 20 minutes or until the eggs are set.

5 Serve carefully in the baking dishes. Or if you like, loosen the toast around the edges with 2 forks and lift the toast baskets onto platter.

Fried Egg

1 egg.

Utensils	Ingredients
Small skillet	Butter, margarine or bacon drippings
Saucer	
Long-handled spoon	1 egg
Pancake turner (if you like)	Salt
	Pepper

1 Heat a thin layer of butter in skillet over medium-high heat. Break 1 egg into saucer and carefully slip the egg into the hot butter. Reduce heat.

2 Cook over low heat, spooning the butter over the egg, until the white is set and a film forms over the yolk. The egg is now cooked sunny-side up.

3 If you like, turn the egg over gently with pancake turner and cook a little more. Now the egg is cooked over easy. Sprinkle with salt and pepper before serving.

VARIATION

Poached-fried Egg: Follow recipe for Fried Egg except—cook the egg over low heat until the edge turns white. Add ½ teaspoon water and cover. Cook until the white is set and a film forms over the yolk.

Whenever you're cooking something on the range, it's smart to fit your pan size to the burner size—don't put a small pan on a great big burner! And for safety, turn pan handles so they don't stick out over the edge of the range, but make sure that they're not over another burner.

Tuna Casserole

6 servings.

Utensils	Ingredients
2-quart casserole with cover	1 package (about 7 ounces) macaroni shells
Large saucepan	3 tablespoons instant minced onion or ½ cup frozen chopped onion
Colander	1 celery stalk
Cutting board	1 package (8 ounces) pasteurized process cheese spread (loaf shape)
Sharp knife	1 can (12½ ounces) tuna
Fork	1 can (10¾ ounces) condensed cream of chicken soup
Long-handled spoon	Milk
	1 jar (2 ounces) sliced pimiento
	1 teaspoon bottled lemon juice

1 Heat oven to 375°. Grease casserole with shortening.

2 Cook the macaroni shells as directed on package.* Ask someone older to drain the shells for you. Pour them into the greased casserole. Sprinkle with 3 tablespoons minced onion.

3 Wash 1 celery stalk and pinch off leaves. Chop the celery into ½-inch pieces on cutting board. (If you like more crunch, cut up another celery stalk.) Add the cut-up celery to the macaroni shells and onion.

4 Cut about four ½-inch slices from the cheese loaf. Cut each slice into ½-inch squares until you have enough to measure 1 cup. Empty into the casserole. (Don't put the cheese away—you'll need it later.)

5 Empty the tuna into the colander to drain. Break the tuna into chunks with fork. Add to the casserole and stir. Pour the soup into the casserole. Fill the soup can half full with milk and stir with fork to get all the soup out. Pour the milk into the casserole.

6 Drain the jar of pimiento. Empty the pimiento into the casserole. Sprinkle with 1 teaspoon lemon juice and stir lightly until all ingredients are mixed.

7 Slice thin slices from remaining cheese loaf (enough to cover the top of the casserole). Place the slices on top of the casserole. Cover the casserole.

8 Bake in 375° oven 30 minutes. Uncover and bake 5 minutes.

* Or here's an easy way to cook the macaroni: Drop it into 6 cups rapidly boiling salted water (4 teaspoons salt). Heat until it boils rapidly again. Cook, stirring constantly, 3 minutes. Cover tightly, remove from the heat and let stand 10 minutes. Drain.

Note: In place of the cream of chicken soup, you can use 1 can (10¾ ounces) condensed cream of shrimp soup.

Tuna Chow Mein

6 to 8 servings.

Utensils	Ingredients
Cutting board	1 can (8 ounces) water
Sharp knife	chestnuts
Jelly roll pan,	1 can (16 ounces)
15½ × 10½ × 1 inch	Chinese vegetables
Large saucepan	1 jar (2 ounces) sliced
Long-handled spoon	pimiento
Colander	3 celery stalks
Fork	6 cups chow mein
Small bowl	noodles (about 12
6 to 8 dinner plates	ounces)
	1 can (13¾ ounces)
	condensed chicken
	broth
	3 tablespoons instant
	minced onion or ½
	cup frozen chopped
	onion
	3 tablespoons soy sauce
	1 can (12½ ounces)
	tuna
	3 tablespoons cornstarch
	¼ cup water
	1 can (11 ounces)
	mandarin orange
	segments

1 Heat oven to 150°.

2 Drain the cans of water chestnuts and Chinese vegetables and the jar of pimiento.

3 Wash 3 celery stalks and pinch off leaves. (Feed them to the hamsters or add to a soup for extra flavor.) Chop the celery into ½-inch pieces and cut the water chestnuts into ¼-inch slices on cutting board.

4 Spread 6 cups chow mein noodles in ungreased jelly roll pan. Heat in 150° oven while you prepare the chow mein.

5 Stir together the Chinese vegetables, pimiento, celery, water chestnuts, broth, 3 tablespoons minced onion and 3 table-spoons soy sauce in saucepan. Heat to boiling over medium heat, stirring occasionally. Reduce heat and simmer uncovered over low heat 1 minute.

6 Empty the tuna into colander to drain. Break the tuna into chunks with fork.

7 Mix in bowl with fork 3 tablespoons cornstarch and ¼ cup water until smooth. Stir into the chow mein mixture. Cook until mixture thickens and boils, stirring constantly. Stir in the tuna chunks. Boil and stir 1 minute.

8 Place about 1 cup of the hot chow mein noodles on each dinner plate. Top with the chow mein.

9 Drain the can of orange segments. Garnish each plate of chow mein with a few segments.

Cook's Corner

The easiest way to drain liquid from cans (but be careful!) is to open the can almost all the way around. Hold the fingers of one hand over the lid (to keep the solids from falling out) and turn the can upside down until the liquid has drained out. Then finish opening the can. (If you want to save the liquid, drain the can over a bowl.)

This method is good for things like tuna fish and vegetables that go into casseroles, which are rather moist anyway. If fruit from cans has to be very dry (as in Sprinkle Cookies, page 24, or Pineapple-Ham Haystacks, page 69), drain the can, then spread the fruit out on paper towels to dry.

Baked Fish with Onion Rings

6 servings.

Utensils	Ingredients
Cutting board	2 packages (1 pound each) frozen skinless haddock fillets
Sharp knife	½ teaspoon salt
Oblong baking pan, 13 × 9 × 2 inches	2 tablespoons bottled lemon juice
Pancake turner	1 can (11 ounces) condensed Cheddar cheese soup
Fork	½ teaspoon paprika
	1 package (9 ounces) frozen French fried onions
	3 dill pickles

1 Heat oven to 475°.

2 Let the frozen fillets stand at room temperature 10 minutes for easier cutting.

3 Cut the fillets into 6 blocks of equal size on cutting board.

4 Place the blocks in ungreased baking pan. Sprinkle the blocks with ½ teaspoon salt and drizzle with 2 tablespoons lemon juice, making sure to get a little of each on each block of fish.

5 Turn the blocks over with pancake turner so salted sides are down. Separate each block from the others.

6 Stir the soup in the can with fork and pour it evenly over the blocks. Sprinkle with ½ teaspoon paprika. Cover with the frozen onions.

7 Bake uncovered in 475° oven 25 to 30 minutes or until the fish flakes easily with the fork and the onions are crisp.

8 While the fish is baking, cut each pickle crosswise into 5 or 6 slices.

9 Arrange 2 or 3 pickle slices on each serving.

Note: In place of the Cheddar cheese soup, you can use 1 can (10¾ ounces) condensed cream of shrimp soup. Omit the pickles.

Here are a few fishy facts:

Is fish really "brain food"? No. Eating fish won't make you any smarter, but you're smart if you eat fish. It's full of valuable protein and minerals to help you grow and stay healthy.

What are fish fillets? They're the sides of the fish, cut away from the backbone. Fillets are practically boneless.

What are fish sticks? They're "sticks" of fish that have been cut from frozen blocks of fish fillets. They're coated with batter, dipped in a crumb mixture, partly cooked, then frozen. You finish the cooking and serve them with fondue or in taco shells or other ways.

Do fish need lots of cooking? No! They're very tender to start with.

Crispy Fried Fish

3 or 4 servings.

Utensils	Ingredients
Small bowl	1 cup milk
Spoon	2 teaspoons salt
Pie pan	1 cup white cornmeal
Large skillet	¼ cup salad oil
Tongs	1 pound fish fillets*
Paper towels	

1 Mix 1 cup milk and 2 teaspoons salt in small bowl. Empty 1 cup cornmeal into pie pan.

2 Heat ¼ cup oil in skillet over medium heat.

3 Dip each fillet in the milk, then in the cornmeal with tongs. Place the coated fillets in the hot skillet and fry about 5 minutes on each side. (Do not overcook.)

4 Drain on paper towels.

* Haddock, pike, trout, perch, sunfish or crappies are all good fish to use.

Note: In place of the cornmeal, you can use 1 cup biscuit baking mix.

This is a good way to cook freshly caught fish at home or over a campfire.

Fish Stick Fondue

6 servings.

Utensils	Ingredients
Cutting board	2 packages (7 or 8 ounces each) frozen breaded fish sticks
Sharp knife	
Cookie sheet or jelly roll pan, 15½ × 10½ × 1 inch	1 large dill pickle
	½ cup mayonnaise or salad dressing
2 small serving bowls	½ teaspoon onion powder
Fork	
Pancake turner	½ cup chili sauce
Serving platter	1 teaspoon horseradish
Fondue forks or wooden picks	1 teaspoon bottled lemon juice
	¼ teaspoon Worcestershire sauce
	Dash of salt

1 Heat oven to temperature given on fish stick package. Let the frozen fish sticks stand at room temperature 10 minutes for easier cutting.

2 Cut each fish stick crosswise into 3 equal pieces on cutting board. Place the fish stick pieces on ungreased cookie sheet.

3 Chop 1 pickle into ¼-inch pieces. Mix the chopped pickle, ½ cup mayonnaise and ½ teaspoon onion powder in serving bowl with fork.

4 Mix ½ cup chili sauce, 1 teaspoon horseradish, 1 teaspoon lemon juice, ¼ teaspoon Worcestershire sauce and dash of salt in another serving bowl with fork.

5 Bake the fish stick pieces as directed on package. Lift to platter with pancake turner. Serve the fish stick pieces with the 2 bowls of dips, along with fondue forks.

Taco-Taco Fish Sticks

10 tacos.

Utensils	Ingredients
Cutting board	Lettuce wedge (about 2 inches thick)
Sharp knife	1 can (6 ounces) tomato paste
3 small serving bowls	
Fork	1 teaspoon water
2 cookie sheets	1 package (4 ounces) shredded Cheddar cheese (about 1 cup)
Pancake turner	
2 serving platters	
	1 package (7 or 8 ounces) frozen breaded fish sticks
	1 package (5 ounces) taco shells (10 shells)
	Bottled taco sauce

1 Heat oven to temperature given on fish stick package. Chop the lettuce into shreds on cutting board. Place in serving bowl.

2 Mix the tomato paste and 1 teaspoon water in another serving bowl with fork.

3 Empty the shredded cheese into another serving bowl.

4 Place the fish sticks on ungreased cookie sheet. Bake as directed on package.

5 Place the taco shells on another ungreased cookie sheet. Three minutes before the fish sticks are done, place the taco shells in oven to heat. Lift the fish sticks and taco shells to platters with pancake turner.

6 Serve the fish sticks and taco shells along with the lettuce, tomato paste mixture and cheese. Let each person at the table make his or her own taco combination. Pass taco sauce.

Pictured: Watermelon Star Salad (page 112)

SUPER SALADS AND VEGETABLES

Friendly Dog Salad

1 salad.

Utensils	Ingredients
Paper towels	1 lettuce leaf
Salad plate	1 canned pear half
Fork	1 canned prune
Kitchen scissors	2 canned mandarin
Teaspoon	orange segments
	1 maraschino cherry
	1 raisin

1   Wash 1 lettuce leaf and pat dry with paper towel. Place on salad plate. Lift 1 pear half, 1 prune and 2 mandarin orange segments from cans and 1 maraschino cherry from jar with fork and place on paper towel to dry. (Refrigerate remaining fruit with syrup for another time.)

2   Place the pear half cut side down on the lettuce leaf. Cut the prune lengthwise in half with scissors and take out pit. Place one of the prune halves at the large end of the pear half for the ear. (Eat the other prune half!)

3   Scoop out a tiny hole in the pear half for the eye with teaspoon. Place 1 raisin in the hole. Cut the maraschino cherry in half with the scissors. Place one half at the top of the narrow end of the pear half for the nose. (Eat the other cherry half!) Use the mandarin orange segments for the collar.

Fruits on Skewers

1 Place a pineapple chunk, a mandarin orange segment, a watermelon pickle and a maraschino cherry or a grape on a skewer. If there is room, repeat the fruits. Leave a little space on each end of the skewer. Repeat until you've filled as many skewers as you want with fruit.

2 Cut a thin slice from the stem end of an orange (so it won't roll around) and place the orange cut side down on a small plate. Poke the skewers into the orange. To eat the fruit, push it off the skewer with a fork.

Yellow-Haired Girl Salad

1 salad.

Utensils	Ingredients
Paper towels	1 ruffly lettuce leaf
Fork	1 canned peach half
Cutting board	1 maraschino cherry
Sharp knife	1 celery stalk
Salad plate	1 large marshmallow
Kitchen scissors	10 raisins
	Shredded yellow cheese

1 Wash 1 lettuce leaf and pat dry with paper towel. Lift 1 peach half from can and 1 maraschino cherry from jar with fork and place on paper towel to dry. (Refrigerate remaining peaches and cherries with syrup for another time.)

2 Wash 1 celery stalk and pinch off leaves. Cut the celery into thin strips about 2 inches long and ¼ inch wide on cutting

board. Keep 4 strips for your salad. (Refrigerate the rest for nibbles.)

3 Place the peach half cut side down in center of salad plate. Place 1 marshmallow at one end of the peach half for the head.

4 Place the celery strips at the sides and bottom of the peach half for arms and legs. Place 1 raisin at the end of each strip for hands and feet. Use raisins for eyes, nose and buttons too.

5 Place some shredded cheese around the marshmallow for hair. Cut a piece off the maraschino cherry with scissors to make mouth and place on marshmallow. (Eat the rest of the cherry!)

6 Now all your salad girl needs is a skirt, so tear a ruffly edge off the lettuce leaf and dress her with it. (Eat the rest of the lettuce or save it for the hamsters.)

Ham Roll-Ups with Cantaloupe Wedges

4 servings.

Utensils	Ingredients
Wooden picks	4 thin slices cooked lean
Sharp knife	smoked ham or
Spoon	4 slices bologna
	1 small cantaloupe

1 Roll up each slice of ham as tightly as you can. Fasten with wooden picks.

2 Cut the cantaloupe into 4 wedges. Scoop out the seeds. Serve a ham roll with each melon wedge.

Firecracker Salads

6 salads.

Utensils	Ingredients
Cutting board	1 package (10 ounces)
Sharp knife	frozen sliced straw-
Small saucepan	berries
2 small bowls	1 celery stalk
Long-handled spoon	1 cup water
Fork	1 package (3 ounces)
6 glasses (about 6	strawberry-flavored
ounces each)	gelatin
Rubber scraper	½ cup frozen whipped
Tablespoon	topping, thawed
	½ cup miniature marsh-
	mallows
	½ cup blueberries

1 Remove the strawberries from freezer. Let stand at room temperature about 10 minutes so they thaw slightly.

2 Wash 1 celery stalk and pinch off leaves. Cut the celery into thin strips about 2 inches long and ¼ inch wide on cutting board. Keep 6 strips for your salads. (Refrigerate the rest for nibbles.)

3 Heat 1 cup water just to boiling in saucepan over medium-high heat. Empty the gelatin into bowl. Pour the boiling water over the gelatin. Stir until the gelatin dissolves. Stir in the slightly thawed strawberries. Break apart the clumps of strawberries with fork.

4 Pour the gelatin-strawberry mixture into 6 glasses, filling each glass about ⅓ of the way to the top. Refrigerate at least 2 hours or until the gelatin is firm.

5 Just before serving, empty ½ cup whipped topping into another bowl. Fold in ½ cup miniature marshmallows. Spoon about

2 tablespoons of the topping mixture onto the gelatin in each glass. Top with about 1 tablespoon blueberries. Poke 1 celery strip into the top of each salad to make the firecracker's fuse.

Watermelon Star Salad
Pictured on page 109.

1 salad.

Utensils	Ingredients
Paper towel	Lettuce leaf
Salad plate	½ slice medium water-
Cutting board	melon (1 inch thick)
Sharp knife	½ cup creamed cottage
Tablespoon	cheese
	1 tablespoon blueberries

1 Wash 1 lettuce leaf and pat dry with paper towel. Place on salad plate.

2 Cut the watermelon slice into 5 wedges on cutting board. Cut the red melon away from the white part and green rind.

3 Arrange the melon wedges on the lettuce leaf in a circle with the points outward to make a star. Spoon ½ cup cottage cheese into the center of the watermelon star.

4 Sprinkle the cottage cheese with 1 tablespoon blueberries.

Porcupine Salads

6 salads.

Utensils	Ingredients
Paper towels	6 lettuce leaves
6 salad plates	6 canned peach halves
Fork	12 maraschino cherries
Kitchen scissors	1 package (3 ounces)
Small bowl	cream cheese,
Teaspoon	softened*
	12 grapes
	Slivered almonds

1   Wash 6 lettuce leaves and pat dry with paper towels. Place 1 lettuce leaf on each salad plate. Lift 6 peach halves from can with fork and place on paper towels to dry. (Refrigerate remaining peaches with syrup for another time.)

2   Cut 12 maraschino cherries into small pieces with scissors and empty into bowl. Stir in the cream cheese with fork and mix until blended. Drop a teaspoonful of the mixture onto the center of each lettuce leaf. Place a peach half cut side down to cover the mixture on each lettuce leaf.

3   Cut 6 grapes into 4 pieces each with the scissors. Place 4 pieces around each peach half for feet. Use 1 uncut grape for the head of each porcupine. Poke a few slivered almonds into the top of each peach half to look like porcupine quills.

* You can soften cream cheese the way you do butter—let it stand at room temperature for about an hour.

Note: You can change the porcupine salad to look like a prehistoric stegosaurus. Put the slivered almonds in a single row on the peach to look like rows of bony plates along a stegosaurus's spine.

Crunchy Coleslaw

4 or 5 servings.

Utensils	Ingredients
Cutting board	1 small head cabbage
Sharp knife	1 medium red apple
Medium bowl	1 cup miniature marsh-
Apple corer	mallows
Fork	1 teaspoon bottled
	lemon juice
	½ cup pineapple, lemon
	or lime yogurt
	2 tablespoons chopped
	nuts

1   Chop the cabbage into long shreds on cutting board, then chop the shreds into small pieces until you have enough to measure 2 cups. Place in bowl. (Wrap remaining cabbage and refrigerate to use another time.)

2   Wash and core 1 apple. Cut into quarters. Chop each quarter into ¼-inch pieces. Place in the bowl. Add 1 cup miniature marshmallows, 1 teaspoon lemon juice and ½ cup yogurt and toss with fork.

3   Sprinkle with 2 tablespoons chopped nuts.

Note: To shred cabbage in the blender, cut half the cabbage into 2-inch pieces and place in the blender container. Add cold water just to cover the cabbage. Cover the blender and follow the manufacturer's instructions or run just long enough to chop the cabbage, 3 to 4 seconds. Drain thoroughly and measure. Repeat with remaining cabbage if necessary to make 2 cups.

Italian Salads with Bambinos

4 salads.

Utensils	Ingredients
Paper towels	Bambinos (right)
4 salad plates	4 lettuce leaves
or trays	12 cherry tomatoes
Sharp knife	8 radishes
Table knife	3 tablespoons cream
12 wooden picks	cheese (about half a
Cutting board	3-ounce package)
Pancake turner	4 slices bologna (about
Serving platter	4 inches across)
Small serving bowl	¼ pound mozzarella or
	Cheddar cheese
	4 sweet pickles
	Bottled Italian salad
	dressing

1 Prepare Bambinos but do not bake them.

2 Wash 4 lettuce leaves and pat dry with paper towels. Place 1 leaf on each salad plate. Wash 12 cherry tomatoes and wash and trim 8 radishes.

3 Spread a little more than 2 teaspoons cream cheese on each bologna slice. Roll up and fasten each with wooden pick.

4 Heat oven to 400°.

5 Cut the mozzarella cheese into 8 cubes on cutting board. Poke a wooden pick into each cube. Make lengthwise cuts in 4 pickles almost to the ends to make fans.

6 Place 1 bologna roll-up, 3 cherry tomatoes, 2 radishes, 2 cubes of cheese and 1 pickle fan on each lettuce leaf.

7 Heat the Bambinos in 400° oven 3 to 5 minutes or until the cheese melts. Lift the Bambinos to platter with pancake turner.

8 Pour some salad dressing into small bowl. Serve the dressing and Bambinos with the salads.

Bambinos

Utensils	Ingredients
Small bowl	¼ cup tomato paste
Fork	¼ teaspoon garlic salt
Cookie sheet	¼ teaspoon oregano
Spatula	18 round snack
Cutting board	crackers
Sharp knife	3 thin slices hard
	salami (about 4
	ounces)
	⅓ cup shredded Cheddar
	cheese

1 Mix ¼ cup tomato paste, ¼ teaspoon garlic salt and ¼ teaspoon oregano in bowl with fork.

2 Arrange 18 crackers on ungreased cookie sheet. Spread about 1 teaspoon tomato paste mixture on each cracker with spatula.

3 Cut each salami slice into 6 pieces on cutting board. Top each cracker with 1 salami piece.

4 Sprinkle the salami with ⅓ cup shredded cheese. Now go back to Step 2 of the salad recipe.

Note: Shredded cheese is moist and comes in packages. Grated cheese is dry and comes in shaker cans.

Volcano Salads

4 main-dish salads.

Utensils	Ingredients
Cutting board	1 medium head lettuce
Sharp knife	4 strawberries
Paper towels	1 pound cooked lean
Spoon	smoked ham
4 salad bowls	1 pound provolone or
	Cheddar cheese
	½ cantaloupe
	Lava Dressing (right)

1 Cut core from the lettuce on cutting board. Rinse the lettuce under running cold water. Save 8 nice leaves. (You'll use these later.) Throw away any bruised leaves. Tear remaining lettuce into bite-size chunks. Place the chunks on paper towels to dry.

2 Wash 4 strawberries (do not remove stems) and place on paper towels to dry.

3 Cut the ham and the cheese each into 16 to 20 strips about 4 inches long and ½ inch wide.

4 Cut ½ cantaloupe into 8 wedges. Scoop out the seeds. Pare the wedges and cut each crosswise in half.

5 Place 2 lettuce leaves in each salad bowl. Mound the lettuce chunks in a pyramid shape on the leaves.

6 Place 4 or 5 strips of ham and 4 or 5 strips of cheese around each lettuce mound to look like the sides of a volcano. Arrange 4 cantaloupe pieces around each mound.

7 Prepare Lava Dressing.

8 Top each salad with a spoonful of dressing and 1 strawberry.

Lava Dressing

Utensils	Ingredients
Small bowl	⅓ cup mayonnaise or
Fork	salad dressing
	2 tablespoons chili sauce
	⅛ teaspoon oregano
	leaves

Mix all ingredients in bowl with fork. Now go back to Step 8.

Note: This makes 4 very generous main-dish salads. If you like, you can divide the ingredients among 6 salad bowls instead of 4 and double the amount of Lava Dressing.

Cook's Corner

Lettuce is almost everybody's favorite rabbit food. It's a big part of most salads, and it tastes the very best when it's fresh and crisp.

To prepare lettuce leaves (sometimes called cups), use a sharp knife to cut the core from the head. To rinse the lettuce and loosen the leaves, hold the head cut side up under running cold water. Then separate the leaves and pat them dry.

Chicken-Bacon-Lettuce-Tomato Salads

4 main-dish salads.

Utensils	Ingredients
Cutting board	2 celery stalks
Sharp knife	2 cans (5 ounces each)
Colander	boned chicken
Fork	⅓ cup mayonnaise or
Medium bowl	salad dressing
Rolling pin (if you	½ teaspoon instant
like)	minced onion*
Rubber scraper	1 snack-size package
Paper towels	(⅝ ounce) potato
4 salad plates	chips
Spoon	4 lettuce leaves
	Bacon-flavored vegetable
	protein chips
	2 medium tomatoes

1 Wash 2 celery stalks and pinch off leaves. Chop the celery into ¼-inch pieces on cutting board.

2 Empty the chicken into colander to drain. Break the chicken into chunks with fork and empty into bowl.

3 Stir in the chopped celery, ⅓ cup mayonnaise and ½ teaspoon instant minced onion with fork.

4 Crush the potato chips in the package firmly with your fist or with rolling pin (be careful not to break or open the bag).** Empty the pieces into the salad and fold in with rubber scraper.

5 Wash 4 lettuce leaves and pat dry with paper towels. Place 1 leaf on each salad plate.

6 Spoon the salad onto the lettuce leaves, dividing it evenly among the 4 leaves. Sprinkle with a few bacon-flavored chips.

7 Wash and cut stem ends from 2 tomatoes. Cut each into 8 wedges. Arrange 4 wedges on each salad.

* Before adding instant minced onion, soak in an equal amount of water 3 to 4 minutes.

** If you don't have a snack-size package of potato chips, crush enough to measure 1 cup.

Cook's Corner

Do you eat 4 servings of fruits and vegetables each and every day? Be sure to include a citrus fruit or its juice (like orange and grapefruit), a deep yellow fruit or vegetable (like apricots and cantaloupe, carrots and winter squash), a dark green vegetable (like beans and broccoli) and something green and leafy (like cabbage and Brussels sprouts). These foods are chock full of important vitamins that help keep your skin healthy and help you to see in the dark.

Fold a piece of terry toweling into quarters and place it in the bottom of a loaf pan.

Saturate the towel with water, then sprinkle it evenly with a single layer of mustard seeds.

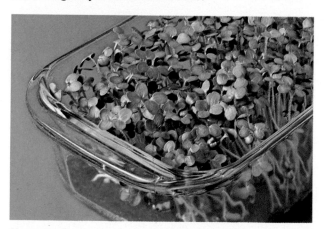
Place the loaf pan in a sunny window, and in 10 to 12 days the tiny plants will be ready to be harvested.

Start Your Own Kitchen Garden

You can grow little plants from the mustard seeds in the kitchen spice cabinet to sprinkle over tossed salads and egg salad, meat and fish sandwich fillings. Try nibbling them all by themselves too—they're good!

1 Fold a piece of terry toweling (about 16 inches long and 8 inches wide) into quarters (about 8 inches long and 4 inches wide). Pat it evenly to cover the bottom of a loaf pan.

2 Pour water over the towel until it's saturated, then sprinkle mustard seeds on top in a single layer.

3 Cover with aluminum foil and leave overnight.

4 Remove the foil and place your planter in a warm, sunny place. Make sure that the towel always stays wet but not covered with water. The seeds will sprout and send roots into the towel. The plants will grow about an inch high, with tiny round green leaves, purple on the undersides, and long, thin stems.

5 Harvest the crop 10 to 12 days after you plant it, snipping the plants off at the base with scissors. (Garden cress, available from seed catalogs, can be grown this way too.)

Salad in a Bag

Pictured on the back cover.

About 6 servings.

Utensils	Ingredients
Cutting board	1 medium head lettuce
Sharp knife	2 medium tomatoes
Paper towels	8 radishes
Plastic bag (about 12 inches long) with fastener	⅓ cup your favorite salad dressing
Large salad bowl	About 6 tablespoons shredded Cheddar cheese

1 Cut core from the lettuce on cutting board. Rinse the lettuce under running cold water. Throw away any bruised leaves. Tear remaining lettuce into bite-size chunks. Place the chunks on paper towels to dry.

2 Wash and cut stem ends from 2 tomatoes. Cut each tomato into 8 wedges. Wash and trim 8 radishes, then cut into thin slices.

3 Place the lettuce chunks, tomato wedges and radish slices in plastic bag. Pour in ⅓ cup salad dressing. (Someone should hold the bag while you pour or pour while you hold the bag.)

4 Close the bag tightly with fastener or hold it closed tightly. Then shake vigorously once or twice. Empty into salad bowl. Sprinkle with about 6 tablespoons shredded cheese.

Garlic Croutons

About 2 cups croutons.

Utensils	Ingredients
Cutting board	4 slices white bread
Sharp knife	Soft butter or margarine
Table knife	¼ teaspoon garlic powder
Cookie sheet	
Long-handled spoon	

1 Heat oven to 400°.

2 Trim crust from 4 slices bread on cutting board.

3 Spread both sides of the bread generously with soft butter. Sprinkle with ¼ teaspoon garlic powder. Cut into ½-inch squares and place on ungreased cookie sheet.

4 Bake in 400° oven 10 to 15 minutes or until golden brown and crisp, stirring occasionally.

5 Cool these crispy bread cubes, store them in a tightly covered container and add them to tossed green salads as you need them. Nice sprinkled over steaming hot soup too.

Beef-Vegetable Soup

8 servings.

Utensils	Ingredients
Cutting board	3 celery stalks
Sharp knife	1 pound beef cubed
Dutch oven with cover	steaks
Pancake turner or	1 tablespoon shortening
tongs	1 package (10 ounces)
Long-handled spoon	frozen whole kernel
	corn
	1 package (9 ounces)
	frozen cut green
	beans
	1 package (9 ounces)
	frozen wax beans
	2 cups frozen sliced
	carrots (about 8
	ounces)
	1 envelope (about 1¼
	ounces) onion soup
	mix
	1 can (8 ounces) stewed
	tomatoes
	4 cups water
	2 teaspoons salt

1 Wash 3 celery stalks and pinch off leaves. Chop the celery into ½-inch pieces on cutting board.

2 Cut the cubed steaks into 1-inch pieces. Melt 1 tablespoon shortening in Dutch oven over medium-high heat. Add the steak pieces and cook, turning with pancake turner, until brown on both sides.

3 Stir in the chopped celery, corn, green beans, wax beans, 2 cups sliced carrots, the onion soup mix, stewed tomatoes (with liquid), 4 cups water and 2 teaspoons salt. Heat to boiling over medium-high heat, stirring constantly. Reduce heat. Cover and simmer over low heat 10 minutes.

Mashed Potatoes

4 to 6 servings.

Utensils	Ingredients
Vegetable parer	6 medium potatoes
Cutting board	Salt
Sharp knife	½ cup milk
Large saucepan with	3 tablespoons butter or
cover	margarine
Fork	¼ teaspoon salt
Colander	Parsley sprigs (if you
Potato masher	like)
Long-handled spoon	
Serving dish	
Scissors	

1 Wash and pare 6 potatoes. Cut each potato in half on cutting board.

2 Using a measuring cup, pour 1 inch of water into saucepan. Keep track of how many cups of water you use, then add ½ teaspoon salt for each cup of water. Add the potatoes. (The water should just cover them.)

3 Cover and cook over medium heat 20 to 25 minutes or until the potatoes are tender when pierced with fork. Ask someone older to drain the potatoes in colander.

4 Return the potatoes to the saucepan and mash with potato masher until no lumps remain. Add ½ cup milk, 3 tablespoons butter and ¼ teaspoon salt. Beat vigorously until light and fluffy.

5 Spoon the potatoes into serving dish. Snip some parsley onto the potatoes with scissors.

Corn on the Cob

Utensils	Ingredients
Large kettle	Ears of sweet corn
Tongs	Sugar
Serving dish	Bottled lemon juice

1 Husk the ears of corn and remove silk just before cooking.

2 Place the ears in kettle. Using a measuring cup, pour in enough cold water to cover the ears. Keep track of how many cups of water you use, then add 1 tablespoon sugar and 1 tablespoon lemon juice for each gallon (16 cups) of water.

3 Heat to boiling over medium-high heat. Boil uncovered 2 minutes. Lift the corn to serving dish with tongs.

Cheese-Scalloped Corn

4 servings.

Utensils	Ingredients
1-quart casserole	1 can (16 ounces) cream-style corn
Spoon	2 eggs
Table knife	½ cup shredded Cheddar cheese
	½ teaspoon salt
	¼ cup dry bread crumbs

1 Heat oven to 350°.

2 Mix the corn, 2 eggs, ½ cup shredded cheese and ½ teaspoon salt in ungreased casserole. Sprinkle with ¼ cup bread crumbs. Bake the corn uncovered in 350° oven 35 minutes.

Buttered Carrot Sticks

4 servings.

Utensils	Ingredients
Vegetable parer	8 medium carrots
Cutting board	Salt
Sharp knife	2 tablespoons butter or margarine
Large saucepan with cover	
Fork	
Slotted spoon	
Serving dish	

1 Wash and pare 8 carrots, then cut lengthwise into ½-inch strips on cutting board.

2 Using a measuring cup, pour 1 inch of water into saucepan. Keep track of how many cups of water you use, then add ½ teaspoon salt for each cup of water. Add the carrots. (The water should just cover them.)

3 Cover and cook over medium heat 18 to 20 minutes or until the carrots are tender when pierced with fork.

4 Lift the carrots to serving dish with slotted spoon. Gently stir in 2 tablespoons butter.

Easy Baked Squash

4 to 6 servings.

Utensils	Ingredients
1½-quart casserole with cover	2 packages (10 ounces each) frozen squash
Table knife	2 tablespoons butter or margarine
Spoon	½ teaspoon salt
	2 tablespoons instant minced onion

1 Heat oven to 425°.

2 Empty the frozen squash into ungreased casserole. Cut 2 tablespoons butter into pieces and dot the top of the squash with the pieces. Sprinkle with ½ teaspoon salt. Cover.

3 Bake in 425° oven 30 minutes.

4 Remove from oven and stir in 2 tablespoons minced onion. Cover and bake 10 minutes.

Best Bean Soup

10 servings (about 1 cup each).

Utensils	Ingredients
Cutting board	1½-pound canned ham
Sharp knife	2 packages (10 ounces each) precooked beans
Large saucepan	¼ cup instant minced onion or ¾ cup frozen chopped onion
Spoon	1 tablespoon sugar
	1½ teaspoons salt
	1 teaspoon celery salt
	1 teaspoon onion powder
	1 teaspoon chili powder
	10 cups water

1 Cut the ham into 1-inch cubes on cutting board.

2 Empty the beans into saucepan and stir in remaining ingredients. Heat to boiling over medium-high heat. Reduce heat. Simmer over low heat 30 minutes.

Pictured: Peach Double Deckers (page 135)

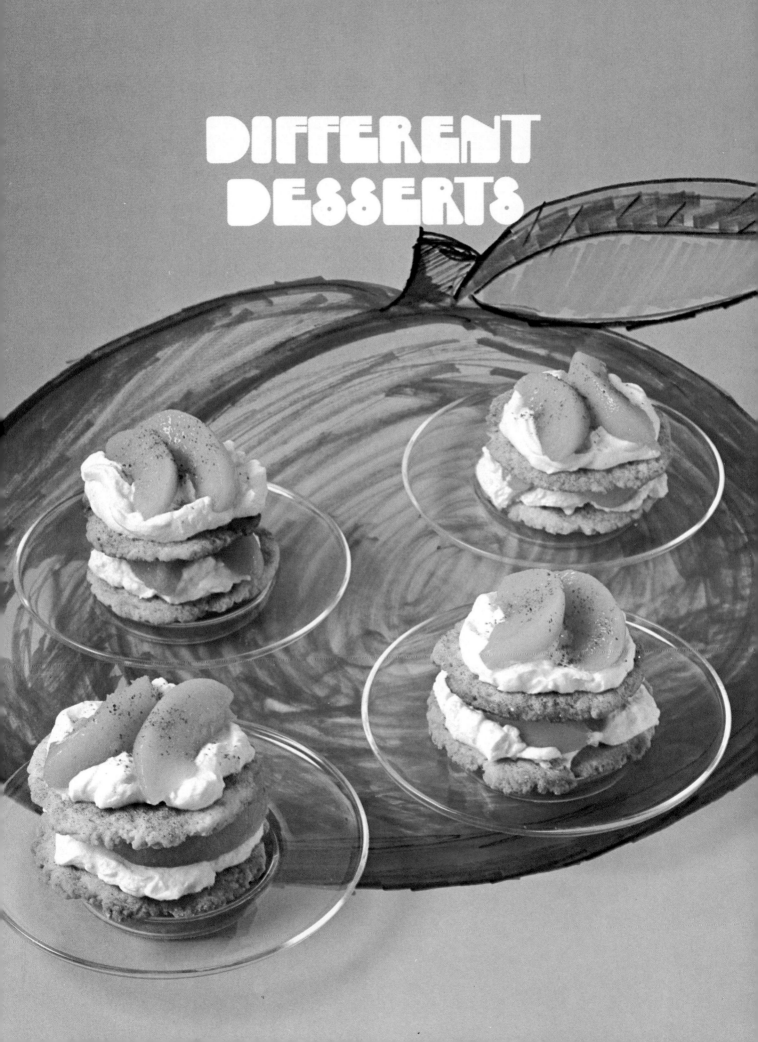

DIFFERENT
DESSERTS

Caramel Applesauce

6 servings.

Utensils	Ingredients
Vegetable parer	6 medium apples
Apple corer	3 tablespoons butter or
Cutting board	margarine
Sharp knife	½ cup brown sugar
Medium saucepan with	(packed)
cover	½ cup water
Long-handled spoon	¼ teaspoon nutmeg
Fork	

1 Wash, pare and core 6 apples. Cut each apple into quarters on cutting board. Cut each quarter into 4 slices.

2 Heat 3 tablespoons butter and ½ cup brown sugar in saucepan over low heat until the butter melts.

3 Remove the saucepan from heat. Stir in the apple slices and mix gently until slices are coated with the butter and brown sugar.

4 Add ½ cup water and ¼ teaspoon nutmeg. (The apples will cook down and add more liquid.)

5 Return the saucepan to heat. Heat to boiling over medium-high heat, stirring occasionally. Reduce heat. Cover and simmer over low heat about 20 minutes or until apples are tender when pierced with fork. Stir once or twice. Serve warm or cold.

Cook's Corner

Superfruit! That's what these jiffy fruit desserts are—superquick to fix, supergood for you and super-delicious to eat!

• Canned fruit cocktail mixed with chopped unpared apple

• Orange slices sprinkled with flaked coconut

• Orange sections arranged like flower petals, with a cherry in the center

• Peach and pear halves with a spoonful of whipped topping, cranberry sauce or your favorite flavor jelly in the centers

• Banana slices mixed with strawberries

• Cantaloupe pieces mixed with grapes

Rhubarberry Sauce

6 servings.

Utensils	Ingredients
Paper towels	2 cups strawberries
Medium saucepan	½ cup water
Long-handled fork	1 package (16 ounces)
	frozen rhubarb
	2 tablespoons sugar
	⅛ teaspoon ginger

1 Wash 2 cups strawberries and remove stems. Place on paper towels to dry.

2 Heat ½ cup water to boiling in saucepan over medium-high heat. Add the rhubarb and 2 tablespoons sugar. Reduce heat. Simmer over low heat 5 minutes, stirring with fork to break the rhubarb apart. Remove from heat.

3 Stir in the strawberries and ⅛ teaspoon ginger. Serve warm or cold.

Puffy Mallow Snowballs

2 snowballs.

Utensils	Ingredients
Toaster	2 frozen round waffles
Cookie sheet	(4½ inches across)
Ice-cream scoop*	⅔ cup chocolate ice
Pancake turner	cream
2 dessert plates	1 cup miniature marsh-
	mallows
	2 tablespoons chocolate-
	flavored topping

1 Toast 2 waffles, then cool about 15 minutes. Place on ungreased cookie sheet.

2 Place 1 scoop of ice cream in the center of each waffle.

3 Quickly place the waffles in freezer. Freeze about 1 hour or until the ice cream is firm.

4 About 10 minutes before serving, heat oven to 500°.

5 Just before serving, take one waffle out of the freezer and press ½ cup of the miniature marshmallows into the ice cream. Return the first waffle to the cookie sheet in the freezer. Take the second waffle out of the freezer and press remaining ½ cup marshmallows into the ice cream. Return the second waffle to the cookie sheet.

6 Bake in 500° oven 3 minutes or until the marshmallows are light brown. Watch every minute so you can take them out as soon as they're ready!

7 Lift the desserts to 2 dessert plates with pancake turner. Drizzle 1 tablespoon chocolate-flavored syrup over each dessert. Serve right away.

* A #16 scoop (about ⅓ cup) is exactly the right size for this recipe. Don't use a larger scoop unless you use a larger waffle. If your scoop is smaller, you may not need as many marshmallows.

Note: The marshmallows and waffles keep the ice cream from melting in the oven.

Raspberry Ice Cream

4 quarts ice cream.

Utensils	Ingredients
Electric ice-cream freezer*	4 packages (10 ounces each) frozen raspberries
Dishpan or roasting pan	2 cups sugar
Blender	2 quarts (8 cups) light cream (20%)
Long-handled spoon	Ice cubes or crushed ice (about 6 quarts)
Large bowl	
Waxed paper (if you like)	About 2 cups rock salt

1 Thaw the frozen raspberries as directed on package.

2 Take ice-cream can (with dasher inside) out of ice-cream freezer and chill it in freezer or refrigerator.

3 Place the ice-cream freezer in dishpan to catch water that will drain from the hole in side of the freezer. Fit the chilled ice-cream can into the freezer. Fit the dasher into place in the can.

4 Empty 1 package thawed raspberries into blender container. Cover and blend on low speed 10 seconds or until the berries are liquid. Pour into the ice-cream can. Repeat, one package at a time, with remaining berries.

5 Empty 2 cups sugar into the ice-cream can. Pour in 2 quarts light cream and stir about 1 minute to dissolve the sugar.

6 Put the cover on the ice-cream can and fasten the top of the freezer with the help of someone older. Drop ice cubes (small ones work best) around the ice-cream can

to a depth of about 3 inches. Sprinkle with ½ cup rock salt.

7 Plug in the freezer. (First be sure your hands are dry!) As the can turns, keep adding a 3-inch layer of ice and ½ cup rock salt around it until the top of the can is covered.

8 As the ice melts, keep adding ice and rock salt for 30 to 40 minutes or until the can starts to turn with difficulty.

9 Pull the plug and disconnect the motor. Lift the ice-cream can out of the freezer and pry off the cover (with the help of someone older). Lift the dasher into bowl. (Now's the time to lick the dasher!)

10 Serve the ice cream now if you like it soft and swirly. If you like firm ice cream, cover the can with waxed paper and freeze 4 hours.

* If you have a crank-type freezer, ask someone older to show you how to operate it. The results will be the same.

VARIATION

Raspberry Refrigerator Ice Cream: Follow recipe for Raspberry Ice Cream except—use only 1 package (10 ounces) frozen raspberries, ½ cup sugar and 1 pint (2 cups) light cream (20%). After blending, pour into ice cube tray. Stir with a fork to break any bubbles. Freeze about 8 hours or until firm.

Frosting Mix Ice Cream

2 quarts ice cream.

Utensils	Ingredients
Spoon	1 package (14.3 ounces)
Large bowl	chocolate fudge,
Ice-cream freezer	lemon or butter pecan
	creamy frosting mix
	2 cups milk
	1 quart (4 cups)
	whipping cream

1 Mix the frosting mix, 2 cups milk and 1 quart whipping cream in bowl.

2 Pour into ice-cream freezer. Freeze as directed for Raspberry Ice Cream (page 127).

Beat-Up Gelatin

4 servings.

Utensils	Ingredients
Small saucepan	2 cups water
Medium bowl	1 package (3 ounces)
Long-handled spoon	your favorite fruit-
Egg beater	flavored gelatin

1 Prepare the gelatin as directed on package except—refrigerate about 2 hours or until very thick but not set.

2 Beat until light and fluffy, 3 to 4 minutes. Serve right away or refrigerate about 30 minutes.

Root Beer Spin

Pictured on the back cover.

2 cups topping.

Utensils	Ingredients
Small bowl	1 cup chilled whipping
Egg beater	cream
	2 tablespoons root beer-
	flavored soft drink mix

1 Refrigerate bowl 20 minutes.

2 Beat 1 cup whipping cream and 2 tablespoons soft drink mix in the chilled bowl until thick and fluffy.

3 Use as a topping for angel food cake or as a filling for cones: Place 6 flat-bottom ice-cream cones in an ungreased baking pan. Spoon about ⅓ cup Root Beer Spin into each cone. Freeze until soft-frozen, about 1 hour.

Note: Sprinkle leftover soft drink mix over vanilla ice cream or over sugar cookies before baking.

VARIATION

Raspberry Spin: Follow recipe for Root Beer Spin except—in place of the root beer-flavored soft drink mix, use 1 package (10 ounces) frozen raspberries, thawed as directed. Instead of beating the thawed raspberries with the whipping cream, stir them in after the cream is whipped.

Marshmallow Custards

6 custards.

Utensils	Ingredients
Six 6-ounce custard cups	1½ cups miniature marshmallows
Oblong baking pan, 13 × 9 × 2 inches	3 eggs
Small bowl	⅓ cup sugar
Egg beater	Dash of salt
Medium saucepan	1 teaspoon vanilla
Long-handled spoon	2½ cups milk
Table knife	Nutmeg

1 Heat oven to 350°.

2 Place custard cups in ungreased baking pan. Empty ¼ cup miniature marshmallows into each custard cup.

3 Beat 3 eggs, ⅓ cup sugar, dash of salt and 1 teaspoon vanilla in bowl.

4 Scald 2½ cups milk in saucepan. Gradually stir the scalded milk into the egg mixture.

5 Dip out the custard with a measuring cup and pour about ½ cup into each custard cup. Sprinkle each with a little nutmeg.

6 Ask someone older to pour very hot water into the baking pan to within ½ inch of the tops of the custard cups and to lift the pan into oven.

7 Bake in 350° oven about 45 minutes or until knife inserted halfway between the center and edge of a custard comes out clean.

8 Ask someone older to remove the pan from oven and to lift the custards out of the water. After the custards are cool enough to handle, refrigerate them.

Note: To scald milk, heat it to just below boiling—small bubbles will form in the milk around the edge of the saucepan.

Creamy Orange Tapioca

4 servings.

Utensils	Ingredients
Medium saucepan	¼ cup sugar
Long-handled spoon	2 tablespoons quick-cooking tapioca
Rubber scraper	1¼ cups orange juice
4 dessert dishes	1¼ cups frozen whipped topping, thawed
	4 maraschino cherries (if you like)

1 Mix ¼ cup sugar, 2 tablespoons tapioca and 1¼ cups orange juice in saucepan. Let stand 5 minutes.

2 Heat to boiling over medium-high heat, stirring constantly. Remove from heat. Cool 20 minutes.

3 Stir tapioca mixture with rubber scraper, then fold in 1 cup of the whipped topping.

4 Divide the tapioca mixture among 4 dessert dishes and top each serving with a spoonful of remaining whipped topping and 1 maraschino cherry.

Blueberry Cobbler

6 to 8 servings.

Utensils	Ingredients
Strainer	1 package (13.5 ounces) wild blueberry muffin mix
Medium saucepan	
Long-handled spoon	
Square baking pan, 9 × 9 × 2 inches, or oblong baking dish, 11¾ × 7½ × 1¾ inches	1 can (21 ounces) blueberry pie filling
	1 tablespoon bottled lemon juice
	1 teaspoon cinnamon
Medium bowl	1 egg
Fork	½ cup milk
Rubber scraper	2 cups vanilla ice cream (if you like)
Ice-cream scoop (if you like)	

1 Heat oven to 400°.

2 Drain the can of blueberries from the muffin mix into strainer over saucepan. (You'll need the drained liquid first.)

3 Stir the pie filling, 1 tablespoon lemon juice and 1 teaspoon cinnamon into the blueberry liquid. Heat to boiling. Pour into ungreased baking pan.

4 Rinse the blueberries quickly under running cold water. Prepare the muffin mix (using the blueberries) as directed on package except—spread the batter evenly over the hot pie filling mixture with rubber scraper.

5 Bake 25 to 30 minutes. Top each serving with 1 scoop ice cream.

Note: To reheat any leftover cobbler, cover the pan with aluminum foil and heat in 350° oven about 10 minutes.

Quick Date Cake

Utensils	Ingredients
Pastry brush	1 package (14 ounces) date bar mix
Square baking pan, 8 × 8 × 2 inches	½ cup hot water
Medium bowl	2 eggs
Spoon	1 teaspoon baking powder
Rubber scraper	
Wooden pick	½ cup chopped walnuts

1 Heat oven to 375°.

2 Generously grease baking pan with shortening, using pastry brush.

3 Mix Date Filling from the date bar mix and ½ cup hot water in bowl. Stir in Crumbly Mix, 2 eggs, 1 teaspoon baking powder and ½ cup chopped nuts. Spread the batter in the greased pan with rubber scraper.

4 Bake in 375° oven 30 minutes or until wooden pick inserted in the center of the cake comes out clean.

VARIATION

Quick Orange-Date Cake: Follow recipe for Quick Date Cake except—mix ½ cup orange marmalade and 1 teaspoon water in small bowl and spread over the warm cake.

Milk Chocolate Brownie Cake

Pictured on the front cover.

Utensils	Ingredients
Pastry brush	1 cup butter or
Jelly roll pan,	margarine (2 sticks)
15½ × 10½ × 1 inch	1 cup water
Large saucepan	⅓ cup cocoa
Long-handled spoon	2 cups all-purpose
Egg beater	flour*
Rubber scraper	2 cups sugar
Wooden pick	1 teaspoon baking soda
Wire cooling rack	½ teaspoon salt
Spatula	2 eggs
	½ cup plain yogurt or
	dairy sour cream
	Cherry Frosting (right)

1 Heat oven to 375°. Grease jelly roll pan with shortening, using pastry brush.

2 Heat 1 cup butter, 1 cup water and ⅓ cup cocoa to boiling in saucepan, stirring occasionally. Remove from heat.

3 Add 2 cups flour, 2 cups sugar, 1 teaspoon baking soda, ½ teaspoon salt, 2 eggs and ½ cup yogurt and beat until smooth. (The batter will be very thin.)

4 Pour the batter into the greased pan.

5 Ask someone to open the oven door for you—that full pan needs 2 hands. Bake in 375° oven 20 to 25 minutes or until wooden pick inserted in the center of the cake comes out clean. Cool the cake on rack.

6 While the cake is cooling, prepare Cherry Frosting. Pour the frosting over the cooled cake and spread with spatula.

* Do not use self-rising flour in this recipe.

Cherry Frosting

Utensils	Ingredients
Kitchen scissors	1 jar (4 ounces)
Paper towels	maraschino cherries
Large saucepan	½ cup butter or
Long-handled spoon	margarine (1 stick)
Egg beater	⅓ cup cocoa
	⅓ cup milk
	1 package (16 ounces)
	powdered sugar (about
	4½ cups)
	1 teaspoon almond
	extract
	Dash of salt

1 Drain the jar of maraschino cherries. Cut each cherry into 6 pieces with scissors. Place the cherry pieces on paper towels to dry.

2 Heat ½ cup butter, ⅓ cup cocoa and ⅓ cup milk to boiling in saucepan, stirring occasionally. Remove from heat.

3 Add the powdered sugar and beat until smooth.

4 Stir in 1 teaspoon almond extract, dash of salt and the cherry pieces. Now continue with Step 6 of the cake recipe.

Pound Cake with Pokey Frosting

Utensils	Ingredients
Pastry brush	1 package (16 ounces)
Loaf pan, 9 × 5 × 3	golden pound cake
inches	mix
Small mixer bowl	⅔ cup water
Electric mixer	2 eggs
Wooden pick	1 cup powdered sugar
Wire cooling rack	½ teaspoon grated
Serving plate	orange peel
Fork or skewer	½ cup orange juice
Small bowl	

1 Heat oven to 325°. Generously grease loaf pan with shortening, using pastry brush. Sprinkle a little flour into the pan and shake gently from side to side until the flour coats the bottom and sides. Empty out remaining flour.

2 Prepare the pound cake mix as directed on package. After mixing, pour the batter into the greased and floured pan.

3 Bake in 325° oven about 1 hour and 15 minutes or until wooden pick inserted in the center of the cake comes out clean. Cool the cake on rack 10 minutes, then remove from the pan to plate. Poke holes ½ inch apart in the top with fork.

4 Mix 1 cup powdered sugar, ½ teaspoon grated orange peel and ½ cup orange juice in small bowl with fork. Pour a little at a time over the top of the cake.

Angel Food Cake with Snowstorm Frosting

Pictured on the facing page.

Utensils	Ingredients
Serving plate	1 angel food or
Spatula or table knife	chiffon cake
	1 carton (4½ ounces)
	frozen whipped
	topping, thawed
	2⅔ cups (two 3½-ounce
	cans) flaked coconut

1 Place the cake on serving plate. Frost the cake with the whipped topping, using spatula.

2 Sprinkle the cake with 2⅔ cups coconut. Refrigerate until serving time.

Note: You can use tinted coconut if you like.

Rocky Road Frosting

Enough to frost 13 × 9-inch cake.

Utensils	Ingredients
Small saucepan	1 can (16½ ounces)
Long-handled spoon	dark Dutch fudge
Spatula	frosting
	1 cup miniature
	marshmallows
	½ cup chopped nuts

1 Heat the frosting in saucepan over low heat until frosting is liquid, stirring constantly. Remove from heat.

2 Stir in 1 cup miniature marshmallows and ½ cup chopped nuts. Pour the frosting over a cooled cake (chocolate, yellow or banana are good) and spread with spatula.

Pictured: Angel Food Cake with Snowstorm Frosting (above) and Chocolate Bunnies (page 36), Peanutty Chocolate Pie (page 140) and Big Fat Cookies (page 25)

BEST CAKE

BEST PIE

BEST COOKIES

Easy Layer Cake Frostings

Bake your favorite flavor layer cake mix in an oblong baking pan, 13 × 9 × 2 inches, as directed on package. Choose one of the following ideas for frosting and decorating the cake:

Chocolate Chip Frosting

1 While the cake is hot, sprinkle it with 2 packages (about 6 ounces each) semi-sweet or milk chocolate chips. Cover with a cookie sheet and let stand 3 to 5 minutes or until the chocolate chips are soft. (The heat of the cake will melt the chocolate.)

2 Uncover the cake and carefully spread the chocolate over cake with a spatula.

Lace Frosting

1 Sift powdered sugar over the top of the cooled cake. Or if you like, place a paper doily on the cake, then sift powdered sugar over it.

2 Lift the doily off onto waxed paper (to catch the sugar). There will be a pretty design on the cake.

Jelly-Coconut Frosting

1 Beat ¾ cup jelly in a small bowl with a fork until syrupy. Spread over the cooled cake with a spatula.

2 Sprinkle about 1⅓ cups (one 3½-ounce can) flaked coconut over the jelly.

Easy Cupcake Frostings

Bake your favorite flavor cake mix in muffin cups lined with paper baking cups as directed on package. Choose one of the following ideas for frosting and decorating the cupcakes:

Choco-Mint Frosting

1 While the cupcakes are hot, place a chocolate-covered mint patty (about 1½ inches across) on each cupcake.

2 Let the heat of the cupcakes soften the mints slightly, then carefully spread over cupcakes with a spatula.

String Frosting

1 Prepare 1 package (7.2 ounces) your favorite flavor fluffy frosting mix as directed. Frost the cooled cupcakes with a spatula.

2 Pour a little liquid food color into a saucer. Dip a piece of white sewing thread into it. Holding the thread at both ends, stretch it tight and press it into the frosting. (It will look like colored string.)

3 Repeat, using a new piece of thread for each new color. Try plaids and stripes!

Peach Double Deckers

Pictured on page 123.

4 double deckers.

Utensils	Ingredients
2 small bowls	1 package (11 or 22 ounces) pie crust sticks
Fork	
Cookie sheet	2 tablespoons water
Custard cup	1 tablespoon granulated sugar
Spoon	
Pancake turner	½ teaspoon cinnamon
Wire cooling rack	1 can (29 ounces) sliced peaches
Egg beater	
4 dessert plates	½ cup chilled whipping cream
	2 tablespoons powdered sugar
	Nutmeg

1 Heat oven to 475°.

2 Take out 1 pie crust stick. (Save remaining for another time.) Prepare pastry for One-crust Pie as directed on package except —do not roll out. Divide the pastry into 8 equal parts. Shape each into a ball.

3 Pat each ball into a 3½-inch circle on ungreased cookie sheet. Prick each pastry circle with fork at ½-inch intervals, making holes big enough so they won't close up when you bake the circles. (This prevents puffing.)

4 Mix 1 tablespoon granulated sugar and ½ teaspoon cinnamon in custard cup. Sprinkle the pastry circles with the sugar-cinnamon mixture.

5 Bake in 475° oven 7 minutes or until light brown. Lift circles to rack with pancake turner. (These can be baked several hours ahead of time.)

6 Twenty minutes before serving the desserts, refrigerate another small bowl. Just before serving, drain the can of peaches.

7 Beat ½ cup whipping cream and 2 tablespoons powdered sugar in the chilled bowl.

8 Place 1 baked circle on each of 4 dessert plates. Spoon some whipped cream mixture and some peaches onto each. Cover with remaining circles and top with remaining whipped cream mixture and peaches. Sprinkle with nutmeg.

VARIATIONS

Fruit Double Deckers: Follow recipe for Peach Double Deckers except—in place of the can of sliced peaches, use 1 can (21 ounces) cherry, peach, apple, raisin or mincemeat pie filling. Do not drain the liquid from the can.

Pudding Double Deckers: Follow recipe for Peach Double Deckers except—in place of the can of sliced peaches, use 1 can (18 ounces) vanilla or chocolate pudding.

Reminder! *Whenever* you use an electric mixer, be sure that it's unplugged and turned to "off" before you put the beaters in or take them out. And you wouldn't *ever* scrape the side of the bowl without turning the mixer off, would you?

Orange Cream Shortcakes

6 shortcakes.

Utensils	Ingredients
2 forks	Orange Cream (right)
Paper towel	1 can (16 ounces)
Medium saucepan	mandarin orange
Large spoon	segments
Cookie sheet	3 tablespoons butter or
Small bowl	margarine
Pancake turner	2⅓ cups biscuit baking
6 dessert plates	mix
Sharp knife	3 tablespoons sugar
Spoon	½ cup milk
	2 tablespoons sugar
	½ teaspoon cinnamon
	Nutmeg

1 Heat oven to 450°.

2 Prepare Orange Cream. Cover and refrigerate. Lift 6 mandarin orange segments from can with fork and place on paper towel to dry. (You'll use these later for a garnish.)

3 Melt 3 tablespoons butter in saucepan over low heat. Remove from heat. Stir in 2⅓ cups baking mix, 3 tablespoons sugar and ½ cup milk with the fork and mix to a soft dough. Drop the dough by 6 large spoonfuls 2 inches apart onto ungreased cookie sheet.

4 Mix 2 tablespoons sugar and ½ teaspoon cinnamon with another fork in bowl. Sprinkle on the dough mounds. Press the tops of the dough mounds with your fingers to flatten them slightly.

5 Bake in 450° oven about 10 minutes or until light brown.

6 Lift each shortcake with pancake turner onto a dessert plate. Split each warm shortcake crosswise with knife. Spoon some of remaining mandarin orange segments and syrup onto the bottom half of each shortcake. Cover with the top halves (cut sides up to soak up the syrup) and top with remaining mandarin orange segments and syrup.

7 Top each serving with about ⅓ cup Orange Cream. Garnish with a mandarin orange segment and sprinkle with nutmeg.

Orange Cream

Utensils	Ingredients
Small mixer bowl	1 cup whipping cream
Electric mixer or	3 tablespoons partially
egg beater	thawed orange juice
	concentrate
	3 tablespoons honey

Refrigerate mixer bowl 20 minutes. Beat 1 cup whipping cream, 3 tablespoons orange juice concentrate and 3 tablespoons honey in mixer bowl until stiff. Now continue with Step 2.

Note: Add 2¼ cans water to the remaining orange juice concentrate and mix as directed on the can for juice.

VARIATION

Strawberry-Orange Shortcakes: Follow recipe for Orange Cream Shortcakes except—in place of the mandarin orange segments, use 2 cups strawberries sweetened with 2 tablespoons sugar.

Cook's Corner

To flute the edges of Fluted Tart Shells (right), put your left thumb and index finger against the rim. With your right index finger, gently push the pastry between your fingers outward. (Reverse the hands if you're left-handed.)

Red and White Trifle

6 servings.

Utensils	Ingredients
1-quart casserole with cover	¼ of 10-inch angel food cake
Small saucepan	1 package (4¾ ounces) raspberry-currant-flavored pudding and pie filling
Long-handled spoon	
Fork	
6 dessert dishes	2 cups water or fruit juice
	6 tablespoons frozen whipped topping, thawed

1 Tear the cake into 1½-inch pieces. Place in ungreased casserole.

2 Prepare the pudding and pie filling as directed on package for pudding.

3 Pour the hot pudding over the cake pieces, lifting pieces with fork to allow pudding to coat each. Cover and refrigerate at least 4 hours.

4 Divide the trifle among 6 dessert dishes and top each serving with 1 tablespoon whipped topping.

Fluted Tart Shells

6 shells.

Utensils	Ingredients
Pencil	1 package (11 or 22 ounces) pie crust sticks
Ruler or compass	
Heavy paper	2 tablespoons water
Kitchen scissors	
Aluminum foil	
Small bowl	
Fork	
Cookie sheet	

1 Draw a 5-inch circle on a piece of heavy paper and cut it out. With the paper pattern, cut out 6 circles of aluminum foil. Heat oven to 475°.

2 Take out 1 pie crust stick. (Save remaining for another time.) Prepare pastry for One-crust Pie as directed on package except —do not roll out. Divide the pastry into 6 equal parts. Shape each into a ball.

3 Place 1 ball in the center of each foil circle. Press evenly with your palm or fingers until the pastry covers the foil and comes just to the edge. Prick with fork at ½-inch intervals, making holes large enough so they will not close up when you bake the shells. (This prevents puffing.) Turn the edge of the foil and pastry up so there is a 1½-inch stand-up rim all around. Flute the edges of the foil and pastry together. Place on ungreased cookie sheet.

4 Bake in 475° oven 8 to 10 minutes or until light brown. Cool on the cookie sheet, then take off the foil.

Note: Fill these pretty shells with fruit, pudding or both and top with whipped topping and maraschino cherries.

Pink Meringue Pie

Utensils
Table knife
8-inch pie pan
Fork
Wire cooling rack
Small saucepan
Long-handled spoon
Rubber scraper

Ingredients
8- or 9-inch frozen
 unbaked pie shell
1 can (21 ounces)
 cherry pie filling
Pink Meringue (right)

1 Heat oven to temperature given on pie shell package.

2 If using 9-inch frozen pie shell, allow it to stand 5 minutes at room temperature. Loosen with knife, then slide the shell into 8-inch pie pan. Ease the pastry to fit around the edge. (If using 8-inch frozen shell, omit this step.) When you prick the pastry with a fork, make holes large enough so they won't close up when you bake the shell. (This prevents puffing.)

3 Bake the pie shell as directed on package for empty baked crust. Cool on rack.

4 Heat the pie filling in saucepan over low heat 5 to 10 minutes, stirring occasionally. Remove from heat. While the filling is heating, make Pink Meringue.

5 Reduce oven temperature to 400°. Pour the hot pie filling into the pie shell. Spoon the meringue around the edges of the hot pie filling and swirl it with rubber scraper. Be careful to seal the meringue to the edge of the crust to prevent shrinking.

6 Bake in 400° oven about 8 minutes or until the peaks of the meringue are a delicate golden brown. Serve warm or cold.

Pink Meringue

Utensils
Small mixer bowl
Small bowl
Electric mixer
Rubber scraper

Ingredients
3 eggs
¼ teaspoon cream of
 tartar
6 tablespoons sugar
½ teaspoon vanilla
10 drops red food color

1 Separate the egg whites from the yolks.* Pour the whites into small mixer bowl. Cover the egg yolks tightly in small bowl and refrigerate to use within a day or two.

2 Sprinkle ¼ teaspoon cream of tartar over the egg whites. Beat on high speed until foamy. Gradually beat in 6 tablespoons sugar, ½ teaspoon vanilla and 10 drops red food color.

3 Continue beating until stiff and glossy, about 5 minutes. Turn off the mixer occasionally and scrape the side of the bowl with rubber scraper. Now go back to Step 5 of the pie recipe.

* To separate an egg, you will need 2 bowls. Hold the egg over 1 bowl. Gently crack the shell in the middle with a knife. With the cracked side on top, pull open the shell. Rock the yolk from one shell half to the other until all the white flows into the bowl. Drop the yolk into the second bowl. If a bit of yolk falls into the white, lift it out with a spoon (be sure to get it all out, or the whites won't beat up properly!)

VARIATION

Blue Meringue Pie: Follow recipe for Pink Meringue Pie except—in place of cherry pie filling, use blueberry pie filling. In place of 10 drops red food color, use 4 drops blue food color and 2 drops red food color.

To separate an egg, crack the shell with a knife, then with the cracked side on top, pull it open.

Rock the yolk back and forth between the shell halves until all the white flows into a bowl.

Beat the egg white mixture until it's stiff and glossy—the meringue should stand up in peaks.

Drop the meringue by spoonfuls onto the hot pie filling, then spread it with a rubber scraper.

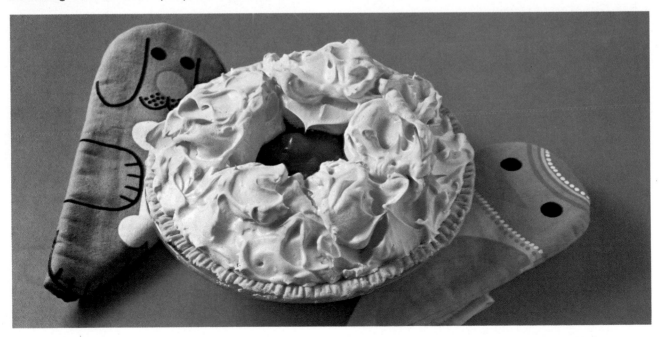

Sherbet Pie in Coconut Crust

Utensils	Ingredients
9-inch pie pan	3 tablespoons butter or
Spoon	margarine, softened
Ice-cream scoop	1½ cups flaked coconut
or large spoon	4 cups lime, raspberry,
	orange or lemon sher-
	bet (or a mixture of
	flavors if you like)

1 Heat oven to 325°. Grease pie pan with 3 tablespoons butter.

2 Press 1½ cups coconut firmly and evenly against the bottom and side of the pan with the back of spoon.

3 Bake in 325° oven 15 to 20 minutes or until golden brown. Cool.

4 Scoop 4 cups sherbet into the cooled crust. Serve right away.

Peanutty Chocolate Pie

Pictured on page 133.

Utensils	Ingredients
Large bowl	1 package (15.4 ounces)
Spoon	chocolate fudge frost-
Cutting board	ing mix
Sharp knife	1 pint (2 cups) chilled
Egg beater	whipping cream
Rubber scraper	Peanut Butter Crumb
	Crust (right)
	½ cup salted peanuts

1 Heat oven to 350°.

2 Mix the chocolate fudge frosting mix

and 1 pint chilled whipping cream in large bowl. Cover the bowl and refrigerate 1 hour.

3 Prepare Peanut Butter Crumb Crust.

4 When the whipping cream mixture has been refrigerated 1 hour, chop ½ cup peanuts into tiny pieces on cutting board.

5 Beat the chilled whipping cream mixture until thick and fluffy, about 1 minute. Fold in the chopped peanuts with rubber scraper.

6 Pour into the cooled crust and freeze at least 6 hours or until firm. Spoon on dabs of whipped topping if you like.

Note: Cut skinny slices of this rich pie!

Peanut Butter Crumb Crust

Utensils	Ingredients
Small saucepan	¼ cup butter or mar-
Fork	garine (½ stick)
Spoon	1½ cups packaged
9-inch pie pan	graham cracker
	crumbs
	¼ cup creamy peanut
	butter
	3 tablespoons sugar

1 Heat oven to 350°.

2 Melt ¼ cup butter in saucepan over low heat. Remove from heat. Stir in 1½ cups graham cracker crumbs, ¼ cup peanut butter and 3 tablespoons sugar with fork.

3 Spoon the mixture into pie pan and press firmly and evenly against the bottom and side of the pan with the back of the spoon.

4 Bake in 350° oven 10 minutes. Cool. Now go back to Step 4 of the pie recipe.

Pictured: Family Breakfast menu (pages 142-144)

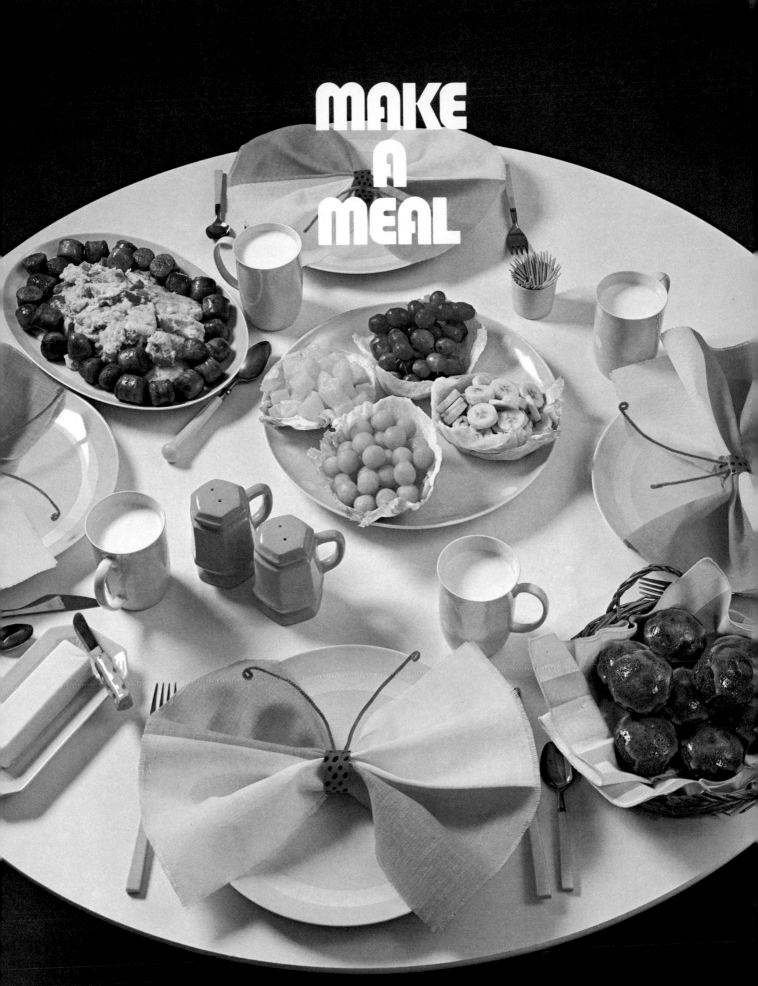

MAKE A MEAL

FAMILY BREAKFAST FOR 4

Bratwurst
Sausage Bites

Shake-Em-Up
Scrambled Eggs

Pick-a-Fruit Platter

Ginger Gems

Milk

Shopping List

1 package (14.5 ounces)
    gingerbread mix
Powdered sugar (1 cup)
Bottled lemon juice (1 teaspoon)
1 small cantaloupe
½ pound seedless green grapes
1 can (8 ounces) pineapple
    chunks in syrup
Lettuce (4 leaves)
1 banana
1 pound precooked bratwurst
    sausage links
1 medium tomato
4 eggs
Shredded Cheddar cheese
    (about 2 ounces)
Shortening (1 tablespoon)
Milk (1 quart)
Butter or margarine (for
    muffins)

Timetable for 10:00 Breakfast

Night before:

1 Prepare Ginger Gems. Spread the tops with Lemon Glaze. Place 9 gems in a square baking pan, 8x8x2 inches, and cover with aluminum foil. (Freeze the remaining gems for another time if you like: Pack in a single layer in a box. Overwrap the box with aluminum foil. Store no longer than 1 month.)

2 Prepare (but do not arrange on the platter) all ingredients except the banana for Pick-a-Fruit Platter. Place the fruits in bowls. Cover and refrigerate. Wrap the lettuce leaves and refrigerate.

Day of breakfast:

8:40 Set the table.

9:00 Finish preparing Pick-a-Fruit Platter except— do not peel or slice the banana into the fourth lettuce leaf.

9:15 Cut up the sausage and place in the skillet.

9:25 Start cooking the sausage.

9:30 Heat oven to 300°. Prepare Shake-Em-Up Scrambled Eggs.

9:45 Place the foil-wrapped pan of gems in oven. Melt the shortening in another skillet and cook the eggs.

9:55 Pour the milk. Peel and slice the banana into the fourth lettuce leaf.

10:00 Arrange the sausage pieces on a platter with the eggs around them. Place the gems on the table. Breakfast is served!

Have you ever made breakfast for your family? Plan it for a lazy day when no one has to jump out of bed and rush off to do things. (Remember that before you make the whole meal, you should always give each recipe a practice run-through in advance.) Make sure you have everything on the Shopping List. Check the Timetable; there are some things for you to do the night before. Then get up, get ready, get the table set and go!

This menu is pictured on page 141. You might like to make the napkin butterflies ahead of time. Here's how: For each butterfly, cut a strip of paper about 6 inches long and 1 inch wide. Color it with felt-tip pens or crayons. Pinch a napkin down the middle and wrap the paper strip around it to make a ring, then tape the paper in place. Poke 2 pipe cleaners into each ring and curve them so they look like a butterfly's feelers.

Bratwurst Sausage Bites

4 servings.

Utensils	Ingredient
Cutting board	1 pound precooked
Sharp knife	bratwurst sausage
Large skillet	links
Pancake turner	

1 Cut the sausage into 1-inch pieces on cutting board.

2 Fry in skillet over medium heat until heated through. Turn the sausage pieces with pancake turner so all sides touch the skillet and brown.

Shake-Em-Up Scrambled Eggs

4 servings.

Utensils	Ingredients
Sharp knife	1 medium tomato
Cutting board	4 eggs
1-quart jar with cover	½ cup shredded Cheddar
Large skillet	cheese (about 2
Pancake turner	ounces)
	½ teaspoon salt
	Dash of pepper
	1 tablespoon shortening

1 Wash and cut stem end from 1 tomato. Chop the tomato into ½-inch pieces on cutting board. Place in jar.

2 Add 4 eggs, ½ cup shredded cheese, ½ teaspoon salt and dash of pepper to the chopped tomato. Cover the jar tightly and shake well.

3 Melt 1 tablespoon shortening in skillet over low heat. Tilt and turn the skillet to coat evenly with the melted shortening.

4 Pour the egg mixture into the hot skillet and cook over medium heat. Turn gently with pancake turner as the mixture starts to set at the bottom.

5 Cook until the eggs are cooked through but are still moist and shiny, 5 to 8 minutes.

Note: In place of the tomato, you can use 1 small celery stalk, chopped, or about ⅓ of a medium green pepper, chopped. Add ¼ cup milk.

This recipe can be doubled for families that love eggs. Use a 2-quart jar with cover to shake the eggs.

Pick-a-Fruit Platter

4 servings.

Utensils	Ingredients
Cutting board	1 small cantaloupe
Sharp knife	½ pound seedless green
Spoon	grapes or red grapes
Melon baller (if you	1 can (13.25 ounces)
like)	pineapple chunks in
Kitchen scissors	syrup
Paper towels	4 curly lettuce leaves
Serving platter	2 bananas
Table knife	
Wooden picks	

1 Cut 1 cantaloupe in half on cutting board. Scoop out seeds and throw them away. Cut the cantaloupe into balls or chunks.

2 Wash the grapes. Cut into small clusters with scissors.

3 Drain the can of pineapple chunks.

4 Wash 4 lettuce leaves and pat dry with paper towels. Arrange the lettuce leaves on platter.

5 Fill each of 3 of the lettuce leaves with a different fruit. Just before serving, peel and slice 2 bananas into the fourth lettuce leaf. Serve with wooden picks.

Ginger Gems

18 gems.

Utensils	Ingredients
2 or 3 muffin pans	1 package (14.5 ounces)
18 paper baking cups	gingerbread mix
(if you like)	1¼ cups lukewarm water
Large mixer bowl	1 egg
Electric mixer	Lemon Glaze (below)
Rubber scraper	Butter or margarine
Wooden pick	
Spatula	

1 Heat oven to 400°. Grease the bottoms of 18 muffin cups with shortening or line with baking cups.

2 Prepare the gingerbread mix as directed on package except—pour the batter into the greased muffin cups, filling each ½ full.

3 Bake in 400° oven about 15 minutes or until wooden pick inserted in the center of a gem comes out clean.

4 Prepare Lemon Glaze. Spread the tops of the warm gems with the glaze, using spatula. Serve with butter.

Lemon Glaze

Utensils	Ingredients
Small bowl	1 cup powdered sugar
Spoon	2 tablespoons milk
	1 teaspoon bottled
	lemon juice

Mix all ingredients in bowl until smooth. Now continue with Step 4.

BACKWARD DINNER FOR 4

Hot Fudge Sundaes
Yummy Pork Chops
Baked Potatoes
Cheesy
Tomato-Bean Bake
Milk
Daisy Salads

Shopping List

Lettuce (4 small leaves)
1 can (16 ounces) peach halves
Maraschino cherries (4)
Celery (1 stalk)
1 carton (12 ounces) creamed
   cottage cheese
Large marshmallows (4)
Colored sugar
4 medium baking potatoes
Salad oil
1 can (16 ounces) cut wax or
   green beans
2 medium tomatoes
Process American cheese
   (4 slices)
4 pork chops, ½ inch thick
Soy sauce (3 tablespoons)
Catsup (3 tablespoons)
Honey (2 teaspoons)
Vanilla ice cream (2 cups)
1 can (16½ ounces) milk
   chocolate frosting
Light corn syrup (1 tablespoon)
Milk (1 quart)
Butter or margarine (for
   baked potatoes)

Timetable for 6:00 Dinner

Day of dinner:

4:15 Prepare Daisy Salads. Refrigerate.

4:35 Heat oven to 350°. Prepare the potatoes for baking.

4:45 Place the potatoes in oven.

4:50 Set the table.

5:00 Prepare Cheesy Tomato-Bean Bake but do not bake.

5:10 Prepare Yummy Pork Chops.

5:25 Place the pork chops in oven. Scoop the ice cream into the dessert dishes. Place in freezer.

5:35 Prepare Hot Fudge Sundae sauce. Remove from heat.

5:55 Place Cheesy Tomato-Bean Bake in oven. Pour the milk. Pour the warm fudge sauce into the pitcher.

6:00 Dinner is served! Place the ice cream on the table and pass the sauce.

6:10 Uncover the pork chops.

6:15 Remove the sundae dishes. Serve the pork chops, potatoes and beans.

6:45 Remove the dinner plates. Serve the salads.

Ice-cream sundaes to start with, then the main course and finally salad—that's how you have a Backward Dinner! Try it sometime when you want to do things a brand-new way. (This menu is pictured on the facing page.)

Hot Fudge Sundaes

4 sundaes.

Utensils	Ingredients
Medium saucepan	1 can (16½ ounces)
Long-handled spoon	chocolate frosting
Ice-cream scoop	1 tablespoon milk
or large spoon	1 tablespoon corn syrup
4 dessert dishes	2 cups vanilla ice cream
Small pitcher	

1 Mix the frosting, 1 tablespoon milk and 1 tablespoon corn syrup in saucepan. Heat over low heat until frosting is liquid, stirring frequently.

2 Scoop 2 cups ice cream into 4 dessert dishes. Serve the hot sauce in pitcher. (Refrigerate leftover sauce. Heat before serving.)

Yummy Pork Chops

4 servings.

Utensils	Ingredients
Cutting board	4 pork chops, ½ inch
Sharp knife	thick
Square baking dish,	3 tablespoons soy sauce
8 × 8 × 2 inches	3 tablespoons catsup
Small bowl	2 teaspoons honey
Spoon	
Aluminum foil	

1 Heat oven to 350°.

2 Cut fat from 4 pork chops on cutting board. Place the chops in ungreased baking dish.

3 Mix 3 tablespoons soy sauce, 3 tablespoons catsup and 2 teaspoons honey in bowl. Pour over the chops. Cover the baking dish with aluminum foil.

4 Bake in 350° oven 45 minutes. Uncover and bake 5 minutes.

Cheesy Tomato-Bean Bake

4 servings.

Utensils	Ingredients
9-inch pie pan	1 can (16 ounces) cut
Sharp knife	wax or green beans
Cutting board	2 medium tomatoes
	Salt
	4 slices process American cheese

1 Heat oven to 350°.

2 Drain the can of beans. Empty into ungreased pie pan.

3 Wash and cut stem ends from 2 tomatoes. Cut the tomatoes into slices on cutting board. Place the slices over the beans. Sprinkle with a little salt. Cover with 4 slices cheese.

4 Bake in 350° oven 20 minutes.

3

2

1

Baked Potatoes

4 servings.

Utensils	Ingredients
Vegetable brush	4 medium white baking
Fork	potatoes
Sharp knife	Salad oil (if you like)
	Butter or margarine
	Salt and pepper

1 Heat oven to 350°.

2 Scrub 4 potatoes with vegetable brush. If you like soft skins, rub with a little salad oil. Prick the skins with fork to let steam escape during baking.

3 Bake in 350° oven 1 hour and 30 minutes. To serve, cut crosswise slits in the potatoes and squeeze each potato until some potato pops up through the opening. Serve with butter and salt and pepper.

Daisy Salads

4 salads.

Utensils	Ingredients
Paper towels	1 ruffly lettuce leaf
Fork	4 canned peach halves
Cutting board	4 maraschino cherries
Sharp knife	1 celery stalk
Spoon	1⅓ cups creamed
4 salad plates	cottage cheese
Kitchen scissors	4 large marshmallows
Glass	Colored sugar
Small bowl	

1 Wash 1 lettuce leaf and pat dry with paper towel. Lift 4 peach halves from can and 4 maraschino cherries from jar with fork

and place on paper towels to dry. (Refrigerate remaining peaches and cherries with syrup to use another time.)

2 Wash 1 celery stalk and pinch off leaves. Cut the celery into thin strips about 2 inches long and ¼ inch wide on cutting board. Keep 4 strips for your salads. (Refrigerate the rest for nibbles.)

3 Spoon ⅓ cup cottage cheese onto center of each salad plate. Place 1 peach half cut side up on each cottage cheese mound.

4 Cut each marshmallow crosswise into 5 pieces with scissors. (Dip the scissors into glass of water to keep the marshmallows from sticking.) Empty a little colored sugar into bowl. Dip the cut sides of the marshmallow pieces into the colored sugar. Arrange 5 pieces in the hollow of each peach half to resemble the petals of a daisy.

5 Place 1 maraschino cherry in the center of each daisy. Use 1 celery strip for the stem of each daisy. If you like, place 1 or 2 celery leaves on each side of the strip.

6 Tear the lettuce leaf into 4 strips and arrange 1 strip at the base of each stem for the grass.

MOM'S DAY DINNER FOR 4

Little Brown Hens

Lettuce
with Dressing

Crunchy
Green Beans

Creamy
Cherry Dessert

Milk

Shopping List

Square cinnamon graham
  crackers (18)
1 envelope (about 1½ ounces)
  whipped topping mix
Milk (1 quart: ½ cup for whipped
  topping, the rest to drink)
Vanilla (1 teaspoon)
1 can (21 ounces) cherry pie filling
Chopped nuts (½ cup)
1 can (16 ounces) French-style
  green beans
1 can (10¾ ounces) condensed
  cream of mushroom soup
4 Rock Cornish hens (about 1
  pound each)
Butter or margarine
  (2 tablespoons)
Worcestershire sauce
  (2 tablespoons)
Soy sauce (1 tablespoon)
Lettuce (½ head)
Instant white or brown rice
  (1½ cups)
Parsley sprigs (5 or 6)
1 can (3½ ounces) French-fried
  onions
Salad dressing (your favorite)

Timetable for 5:00 Dinner

Day before:

1 Prepare Creamy Cherry Dessert. Cover and refrigerate.

2 Mix ingredients for Crunchy Green Beans but do not bake. Cover and refrigerate.

3 Thaw the frozen hens in refrigerator 12 to 16 hours before baking. Continue thawing them at room temperature on the day of the dinner if they need it.

Day of dinner:

2:30 Prepare the Little Brown Hens but do not bake.

2:50 Heat oven to 350°.

3:00 Place the hens in oven.

4:00 Set the table.
Core and wash ½ head lettuce (page 116). Cut into wedges and arrange on salad plates. Refrigerate.

4:25 Place Crunchy Green Beans in oven.

4:30 Measure the ingredients for the rice. Open the can of onions for the beans.

4:45 Take the green beans out of oven. Sprinkle the onions on top and return to oven.

4:50 Cook the rice as directed on package. Pour the milk. Place the lettuce and the dressing on the table.

4:55 Take the hens out of oven and cut the strings. Arrange the rice on the platter. Place the hens on the rice. Place the beans on the table. Dinner is served! (Don't forget the dessert!)

It's Mother's Day, and one of the best ways to make it a pleasant day for your mom is to make her a special dinner. Follow the Time-table carefully, and you'll find that it's easy—and lots of fun.

Making the table look nice is almost as important as making the food taste good. Use pretty dishes, glasses and silverware. And don't forget a centerpiece—it doesn't have to be fancy. What about a few spring flowers in a glass? Or a green plant borrowed from the windowsill? Or a basket or bowl filled with shiny fruits and vegetables in all different colors? Or a cluster of big bright balloons? Or a fat candle? Or see what else you and your imagination can come up with!

Little Brown Hens

4 servings.

Utensils	Ingredients
Paper towels	4 Rock Cornish hens (about 1 pound each)
4 pieces string, each about 6 inches long	
Broiler pan with rack	2 tablespoons butter or margarine
Aluminum foil (if you like)	2 tablespoons Worcester-shire sauce
Small saucepan	1 tablespoon soy sauce
Spoon	1½ cups uncooked instant white or brown rice
Pastry brush	
	Water
Kitchen scissors	5 or 6 parsley sprigs (if you like)
Medium saucepan with cover	
Fork	
Long-handled spoon	
Serving platter	
Pancake turner	

1 Thaw 4 hens in refrigerator 12 to 16 hours before baking.

2 When the hens are thawed, heat oven to 350°.

3 Wash the hens and pat dry with paper towels. Tie the legs of each hen together with a piece of string.

4 Line broiler pan with aluminum foil so the pan will be easy to clean. Place the hens breast sides up on rack in the foil-lined pan.

5 Melt 2 tablespoons butter in saucepan over low heat. Stir in 2 tablespoons Worcestershire sauce and 1 tablespoon soy sauce.

6 Brush the hens generously with the seasoned butter. Save remaining butter for later.

7 Bake in 350° oven 2 hours. Cut the strings and throw away.

8 Prepare 1½ cups instant rice as directed on package. Spoon into 4 mounds on platter.

9 Just before serving, brush the hens again with remaining seasoned butter. Lift the hens onto the rice nests with pancake turner. Garnish with 5 or 6 parsley sprigs.

Before you try any of the special meals in this chapter, it's important for you to make each one of the recipes separately ahead of time. That way you'll learn exactly what you have to do. You'll feel much more relaxed making the entire meal when you're familiar with all the recipes.

Crunchy Green Beans

4 servings.

Utensils	Ingredients
Spoon 1-quart casserole with cover	1 can (16 ounces) French-style green beans 1 can (10¾ ounces) condensed cream of mushroom soup 1 can (3½ ounces) French-fried onions

1 Heat oven to 350°.

2 Drain the can of green beans.

3 Mix the green beans and half of the can of soup in ungreased casserole. Cover.

4 Bake in 350° oven 20 minutes.

5 Remove from oven. Arrange half of the can of onions on top. Bake uncovered 15 minutes.

Note: Cover and refrigerate remaining soup to use the next day. Fill the soup can half full with water and heat as directed. Just before serving, sprinkle remaining onions on top of the soup.

Creamy Cherry Dessert

9 servings.

Utensils	Ingredients
Square baking pan, 9 × 9 × 2 inches Medium bowl Egg beater Rubber scraper Sharp knife	18 square cinnamon graham crackers 1 envelope (about 1½ ounces) whipped topping mix ½ cup cold milk 1 teaspoon vanilla 1 can (21 ounces) cherry pie filling ½ cup chopped nuts

1 Cover bottom of ungreased baking pan with 9 of the graham crackers.

2 Prepare the topping mix as directed on envelope except—before beating, increase the vanilla to 1 teaspoon. Spread the topping over the graham crackers with rubber scraper.

3 Arrange remaining 9 graham crackers over the whipped topping.

4 Spread the pie filling over the graham crackers. Sprinkle with ½ cup chopped nuts.

5 Cover and refrigerate 5 hours or overnight. To serve, cut into squares. (Freeze remaining dessert for another time if you like. Place in refrigerator 30 minutes before serving time.)

DAD'S DAY COOKOUT FOR 6

Sizzling
Hamburgers

Merry-Go-Round
Salad

Gooey French Loaf

Everything Bars

Milk

Shopping List

Butter or margarine (1 cup—
   2 sticks)
Marshmallows (32 large or 3
   cups miniature)
Creamy peanut butter (½ cup)
Instant nonfat dry milk (½ cup)
Orange-flavored instant
   breakfast drink mix (¼ cup)
Raisins (1 cup)
O-shaped puffed oat cereal
   (4 cups)
1 loaf (1 pound) French bread
Frozen chopped onion (¼ cup)
Process American cheese
   (10 slices)
Ground beef (2 pounds)
Lettuce (½ small head)
2 medium tomatoes
1 small cucumber
6 radishes
Imitation bacon chips or cheese-
   flavored croutons (¼ cup)
Salad dressing (your favorite)
Soy sauce (2 teaspoons)
Milk (1½ quarts)

Timetable for 6:00 Cookout

Ahead of time:

1 Prepare, cool and cut Everything Bars.

2 Prepare Gooey French Loaf but do not cook.

Afternoon of cookout:

4:45 Shape the hamburger patties. Separate with squares of waxed paper. Refrigerate.

5:10 Prepare Merry-Go-Round Salad makings. Place in bowls and cover. Refrigerate all but the imitation bacon chips.

5:30 Ask someone older to light the charcoal and watch the fire. Adjust the grill so it is 4 inches from the hot coals. Set the picnic table.

5:40 Place Gooey French Loaf on the grill. Arrange the salad on the lazy Susan.

5:50 Turn the French loaf. Place the hamburgers on the grill.

5:55 Turn the hamburgers. Pour the milk into a large pitcher. Place Everything Bars on the table.

6:00 Place the hamburgers and bread on the table. Picnic time!

Everybody loves cookouts, so this Father's Day why don't you give your dad a big treat and make dinner for him? June is a perfect month for outdoor eating (but cross your fingers and hope that it doesn't rain!).

Make the Everything Bars and get the Gooey French Loaf ready for the grill either the night before or early on the day of the dinner. Then start your cookout countdown.

Windy day tips: Anchor the corners of the tablecloth together with clothespins so it won't flutter around. Get everything ready inside, then set the table at the last minute. Enjoy the meal you've made—and unless you're all *very* hungry, there'll be enough bread and cookies left for another day!

Sizzling Hamburgers

8 burgers.

Utensil	Ingredients
Pancake turner	2 pounds ground beef
	2 teaspoons soy sauce

1 Divide the ground beef into 8 parts. Shape each part into a patty about ¼ inch thick.

2 Place the patties on grill 4 inches from hot coals. Drizzle the patties with 1 teaspoon of the soy sauce, making sure to get a little sauce on each patty.

3 Cook about 4 minutes and turn with pancake turner. Drizzle the other sides of the patties with remaining 1 teaspoon soy sauce. Cook about 4 minutes more. If you're not sure when they're done, ask someone else to help you decide.

Merry-Go-Round Salad

6 servings.

Utensils	Ingredients
Cutting board	Small head lettuce
Sharp knife	2 medium tomatoes
Paper towels	1 small cucumber
Vegetable parer	6 radishes
6 serving bowls	¼ cup imitation bacon
Large lazy Susan	chips or cheese-
platter	flavored croutons
	Your favorite salad
	dressing

1 Cut the lettuce in half on cutting board. Wrap one half and refrigerate to use another time. Cut core from remaining lettuce. Rinse the lettuce under running cold water. Throw away any bruised leaves. Tear remaining lettuce into bite-size chunks. Place the chunks on paper towels to dry.

2 Wash and cut stem ends from 2 tomatoes. Cut each into 8 wedges.

3 Pare 1 cucumber and cut into thin slices. Wash and trim 6 radishes and cut into thin slices.

4 Place the lettuce, vegetables and ¼ cup imitation bacon chips in separate serving bowls and arrange on lazy Susan platter with bowl of salad dressing in the middle. Let everyone choose his or her own salad assortment.

Gooey French Loaf

About 20 slices.

Utensils	Ingredients
Sharp knife	1 loaf (1 pound) French
Small skillet	bread
Spoon	½ cup butter or mar-
Pastry brush	garine (1 stick)
Cutting board	¼ cup frozen chopped
Table knife	onion
Heavy-duty aluminum	10 slices process Ameri-
foil	can cheese
Long-handled tongs	

1 Cut the bread into 1-inch slices almost to the bottom of the loaf.

2 Melt ½ cup butter in skillet. Remove from heat. Stir in ¼ cup chopped onion. Brush the cut surfaces of the bread with the butter-onion mixture.

3 Cut 10 slices cheese diagonally in half on cutting board so you have 20 cheese triangles. Place the cheese triangles between the bread slices.

4 Place loaf in the center of sheet of aluminum foil (about 3 times as wide and 3 inches longer than the loaf). Wrap securely with the foil, twisting ends to make handles for turning.

5 Heat on grill 4 inches from hot coals 10 minutes, turning once with tongs.

Everything Bars

27 bars.

Utensils	Ingredients
Square baking pan,	½ cup butter or mar-
9 × 9 × 2 inches	garine (1 stick)
Large saucepan	32 large marshmallows
Long-handled spoon	or 3 cups miniature
Table knife	marshmallows
	½ cup creamy peanut
	butter
	½ cup instant nonfat
	dry milk
	¼ cup orange-flavored
	instant breakfast
	drink mix
	1 cup raisins
	4 cups O-shaped puffed
	oat cereal

1 Grease baking pan with some butter or margarine.

2 Heat ½ cup butter and 32 large marshmallows in saucepan over low heat until marshmallows melt, stirring constantly. Stir in ½ cup peanut butter until it melts. Stir in ½ cup dry milk and ¼ cup breakfast drink mix. Remove from heat.

3 Stir in 1 cup raisins and 4 cups cereal until coated. Empty into the buttered pan. Rub a little butter on the back of the spoon and use it to pat the mixture evenly in the pan. Cool. Cut into bars, 3 inches long and 1 inch wide.

INDEX

A

Angel Food Cake with Snowstorm
 Frosting, 132
Apple(s)
 Caramel, 51
 -Cheese Snack, 16
 -Cinnamon Coffee Cake, 78
 -Date Softies, 29
 Mallow, in the Coals, 63
 -Sausage Pancakes, 75
Applesauce, Caramel, 124

B

Bacon
 Chicken-, -Lettuce-Tomato
  Salads, 117
 Grilled, 56
Baked
 Cheese Sandwich, 67
 Fish with Onion Rings, 106
 Ham Slice, 97
 Pork Tenderloins, 100
 Potatoes, 148
 Squash, Easy, 122
Banana(s)
 Boats, 17
 Pancakes, 74
 Pick-a-Fruit Platter, 144
 Yum-Yums
  Chocolate-, 16
  Pink or Yellow, 16
Barbecue(d)
 Meat Loaf, 93
 Ribs, Sticky, 100
Basic Meat Loaf, 93
Bean(s)
 Bake, Cheesy Tomato-, 146
 Chili, Texas-Style, 57
 Green, Crunchy, 151
 Refried, Tacos Sealed with, 92
 Soup, Best, 122
 Weenie Dip, 60
Beat-Up Gelatin, 128

Beef
 ground
  Chili, Texas-Style, 57
  Meatballs, Bumpy, 89
  Pizzas, No-Crust Wide-Eyed,
   90
  Sloppy Joes, 88
  Spaghetti, One-Pot Italian,
   89
  Tacos Sealed with Refried
   Beans, 92
 Hamburger(s)
  Dinners in Foil, 96
  Fake Cake, 87
  Juicy, 88
  Open-Face, 68
  Sizzling, 153
 Meat Loaf
  Barbecue, 93
  Basic, 93
  Cheesy, 93
  Flowerpot, 93
  Football, 93
  Horseradish, Zingy, 93
  Rings, 94
  Rings, Potatoes Baked in, 94
 Steak(s)
  Cubed, Chicken-Fried, 87
  Sandwiches, Double, 57
 Stew, Oven Cobblestone, 86
 -Vegetable Soup, 120
Best Bean Soup, 122
Beverages
 Banana-Orange Junior, 19
 Cocoa, 19
 Eggnog, Snowcap, 20
 Foaming Witches' Brew, 39
 Milk, Chocolate, 64
 Orange Sip, 62
 Punch, Bouncing Ball, 43
 Shakes, Purple Cow, 18
 Soda
  Pop, Campers' Foaming, 64
  Strawberry, 20
 Tomato Mush, 23
Big
 Burger Cake, 44–45
 Fat Cookies, 25

Birdseed Bread, 79
Birthday Ice-Cream Cake, 43
Biscuit(s)
 Luncheon Meat-, Bake, 97
 Skillet, Cheesy, 62
 Drop, 62
 Sugar Babies, 62
Blue Meringue Pie, 138
Blueberry(-ies)
 Blue Meringue Pie, 138
 Cobbler, 130
 Waffles, 73
Bologna
 Cups, Eggs in, 102
 Daisies and Macaroni, 101
Bouncing Ball Punch, 43
Bratwurst Sausage Bites, 143
Bread(s). See also Biscuit(s);
  Pancake(s).
 Birdseed, 79
 Butter Dips, 78
 Cheesy Slices, 84
 Coffee Cake, Apple-Cinnamon,
  78
 Dough, Frozen, Fun, 83
 Doughnuts, Hotsy-Totsy, 72
 French Loaf
  Gooey, 154
  Stretchy, 84
 French Toast, 73
 Herbed, in Foil, 63
 Muffins, Surprise, 79
 Pretzels, 80
 Toast
  Coco-Caramel, 72
  Log Cabin, 72
 Waffles, 73
 Wheaten Loaf, 82
Broccoli, Raw Vegetable Snacks,
 23
Brown Sugar Drops, 27
Brownie(s)
 Cake, Milk Chocolate, 131
 Favorite, 26
 Slowpokes, 29
Bumpy Meatballs, 89
Butter Dips, 78
Buttered Carrot Sticks, 121

155

C

Cabbage, Crunchy Coleslaw, 113
Cake(s). See also Cupcake(s).
  Angel Food, with Snowstorm
      Frosting, 132
  Big Burger, 44–45
  Date, Quick, 130
  Ghost, with Flaming Eyes, 39
  Heart, 35
  Milk Chocolate Brownie, 131
  Orange-Date, Quick, 130
  Pound, with Pokey Frosting,
      132
  Pumpkin Loaf, Golden, 37
  Shortcakes
      Orange Cream, 136
      Strawberry-Orange, 136
Campers' Foaming Soda Pop, 64
Candy
  Caramel(s)
      Apples, 51
      Creamy, 48
  Chocolate Bunnies or Chicks,
      36
  Divinity, No-Cook Cherry, 35
  Frosted Pretzels, 52
  Fudge, Rocky Road, 49
  Gumdrop
      Squares, 51
      Trees, 42
  Noodle Nests, 36
  Popcorn Ring Centerpiece, 47
  Taffy, Peppermint, 52
Cantaloupe
  Pick-a-Fruit Platter, 144
  Wedges, Ham Roll-Ups with,
      111
Caramel(s)
  Apples, 51
  Applesauce, 124
  Coco-, Toast, 72
  Creamy, 48
  Fondue, 64
Carrot(s)
  Raw Vegetable Snacks, 23
  Sticks, Buttered, 121
Cauliflower, Raw Vegetable
      Snacks, 23
Celery, Raw Vegetable Snacks, 23

Cheese(-y)
  Apple-, Snack, 16
  Gooey French Loaf, 154
  Meat Loaf, 93
  Pretzels, 80
  Sandwich, Baked, 67
  -Scalloped Corn, 121
  Shake-Em-Up Scrambled
      Eggs, 143
  Skillet Biscuits, 62
      Drop, 62
  Slices, 84
  Tomato-Bean Bake, 146
Cherry(-ies)
  Dessert, Creamy, 151
  Divinity, No-Cook, 35
  Pink Meringue Pie, 138
Chicken
  -Bacon-Lettuce-Tomato
      Salads, 117
  Drumsticks, Glazed, 101
  Noodle Soup, 55
  Quick Chix on Stix, 60
Chicken-Fried Cubed Steaks, 87
Chili
  Foot-Long Coneys, 58
  Texas-Style, 57
Choco-Mint Frosting, 134
Chocolate
  -Banana Yum-Yums, 16
  Brownie(s)
      Cake, Milk, 131
      Favorite, 26
      Slowpokes, 29
  Bunnies or Chicks, 36
  Chip
      Cookies, 26
      Frosting, 134
  Choco-Mint Frosting, 134
  Cocoa, 19
  Fudge
      Hot, Sundae, 146
      Rocky Road, 49
  Milk, 64
  Pie, Peanutty, 140
  S'More, 64
Chow Mein, Tuna, 105
Chunky Tuna Sandwiches, 66
Cobbler, Blueberry, 130
Coco-Caramel Toast, 72
Cocoa, 19

Coconut
  Coco-Caramel Toast, 72
  Crust, Sherbet Pie in, 140
  Jelly-, Frosting, 134
Coffee Cake, Apple-Cinnamon, 78
Coleslaw, Crunchy, 113
Cookie(s)
  Big Fat, 25
  Brown Sugar Drops, 27
  Brownie(s)
      Favorite, 26
      Slowpokes, 29
  Chocolate Chip, 26
  Date Softies
      Apple-, 29
      Pineapple-, 29
      Spicy, 29
  Everything Bars, 154
  Fried Fortune, 34
  Gingersnaps, 24
  Ice-Cream, 28
  Lollipops, 30
  Marshmallow Puffs, 25
  Mexican, 30
  Pick-Your-Flavor, 28
  Pinwheels, 30
  Quick-Energy Pickups, 32
  Root Beer, 27
  Ski Chalet, 40–42
  Sprinkle, 24
  Strawberry Squares, 32
  Teddy Bear Paws, 30
  Yo-Yo, 26
Corn
  Cheese-Scalloped, 121
  in the Coals, 61
  Indian Maize Pancakes, 77
  on the Cob, 121
Cornish hens, Little Brown
      Hens, 150
Crater Ham Loaf, 99
Creamy
  Cherry Dessert, 151
  Orange Tapioca, 129
Crispy Fried Fish, 107
Crunchy
  Coleslaw, 113
  Green Beans, 151
  Peanut Butter, Homemade, 48
Cucumber, Raw Vegetable
      Snacks, 23

Cupcake(s)
　Frostings, Easy, 134
　Ginger Gems, 144
Custards, Marshmallow, 129

D

Daisy Salads, 148
Date
　Cake, Quick, 130
　　Orange-, 130
　Softies
　　Apple-, 29
　　Pineapple-, 29
　　Spicy, 29
Dessert(s). *See also* Cake(s);
　　　Cupcake(s); Ice Cream;
　　　Pie(s).
　Apples, Mallow, in the
　　　Coals, 63
　Applesauce, Caramel, 124
　Blueberry Cobbler, 130
　Caramel Fondue, 64
　Cherry, Creamy, 151
　Custards, Marshmallow, 129
　Fruit Double Deckers, 135
　Gelatin, Beat-Up, 128
　Peach Double Deckers, 135
　Pudding Double Deckers,
　　　135
　Pumpkin Cups, Little, 37
　Raspberry Spin, 128
　Rhubarberry Sauce, 124
　Root Beer Spin, 128
　Tapioca, Creamy Orange,
　　　129
　Tart Shells, Fluted, 137
　Trifle, Red and White, 137
Dillybobs, 58
Dip(s)
　Bean Weenie, 60
　Fondue
　　Caramel, 64
　　Fish Stick, 107
Dit Dit Dot Pancakes, 74
Divinity, No-Cook Cherry, 35
Double Steak Sandwiches, 57
Doughnuts, Hotsy-Totsy, 72
Drinks. *See Beverages.*

E

Easy
　Baked Squash, 122
　Frostings
　　Cupcake, 134
　　Layer Cake, 134
Egg(s)
　Fried, 103
　Hard-Cooked, 66
　in Bologna Cups, 102
　Poached-Fried, 103
　Salad Sandwiches, 67
　　-Peanut, 67
　Scramble(d)
　　Potato-, 56
　　Shake-Em-Up, 143
　Twin, in Toast Basket, 103
Eggnog, Snowcap, 20
Everything Bars, 154

F

Favorite Brownies, 26
Firecracker Salads, 112
Fish
　Baked, with Onion Rings, 106
　Cooked in Foil, 61
　Crispy Fried, 107
　Shrimpy Pizzas, 69
　Stick(s)
　　Fondue, 107
　　Taco-Taco, 108
　Tuna
　　Casserole, 104
　　Chow Mein, 105
　　Sandwiches, Chunky, 66
　　Sandwiches, Hot　66
Float, Rainbow, 19
Flowerpot Meat Loaf, 93
Fluted Tart Shells, 137
Foaming Witches' Brew, 39
Fondue
　Caramel, 64
　Fish Stick, 107
Foot-Long Coneys, 58
Football Meat Loaf, 93
Fortune Cookies, Fried, 34

Frankabobs, 58
Frankfurters
　Bean Weenie Dip, 60
　Dillybobs, 58
　Foot-Long Coneys, 58
　Frankabobs, 58
　Hot Dog Roll-Ups, Toasty,
　　　68
　Polka Dot Pizzas, 71
　Potatobobs, 58
French Toast, 73
Fried
　Egg, 103
　　Poached-, 103
　Fish, Crispy, 107
　Fortune Cookies, 34
　Ham Slice, 97
Friendly Dog Salad, 110
Frosted Pretzels, 52
Frosting(s)
　Cupcake, Easy
　　Choco-Mint, 134
　　String, 134
　Layer Cake, Easy
　　Chocolate Chip, 134
　　Jelly-Coconut, 134
　　Lace, 134
　Mix Ice Cream, 128
　Pokey, Pound Cake with, 132
　Rocky Road, 132
　Snowstorm, Angel Food Cake
　　　with, 132
Frozen Dough Fun, 83
Fruit(s). *See also name of
　　　fruit.*
　Double Deckers, 135
　on Skewers, 111
　Pick-a-, Platter, 144
Fudge
　Hot, Sundaes, 146
　Rocky Road, 49

G

Garden cress, growing, 118
Garlic Croutons, 119
Gelatin, Beat-Up, 128
Ghost Cake with Flaming Eyes,
　　　39

Ginger Gems, 144
Gingerbread
    Cookie Ski Chalet, 40–42
    Ginger Gems, 144
Gingersnaps, 24
Glazed Chicken Drumsticks,
    101
Golden Pumpkin Loaf, 37
Granola, Munchy Crunchy,
    20
Grape(s)
    Jelly, Rosy, 49
    juice, Purple Cow Shakes,
    18
    Pick-a-Fruit Platter, 144
Green Beans, Crunchy, 151
Grilled Bacon, 56
Gumdrop
    Squares, 51
    Trees, 42

H

Ham
    Best Bean Soup, 122
    Kabobs with Red Currant
        Sauce, 98
    Loaf, Crater, 99
    Pineapple-, Haystacks, 69
    Roll-Ups with Cantaloupe
        Wedges, 111
    Slice
        Baked, 97
        Fried, 97
    Volcano Salads, 116
Hamburger(s). See Beef,
        ground; Beef,
        Hamburger(s)
Hard-Cooked Eggs, 66
Hawaiian Pops, 18
Heart Cake, 35
Herbed Bread in Foil, 63
Homemade
    Crunchy Peanut Butter,
        48
    Pancake Syrup, 77
Hot
    Fudge Sundaes, 146
    Tuna Sandwiches, 66

Hot dogs. See Frankfurters.
Hotsy-Totsy Doughnuts, 72

I

Ice Cream
    Banana-Orange Junior, 19
    Cake, Birthday, 43
    Cookies, 28
    Float, Rainbow, 19
    Frosting Mix, 128
    Pink Elephant Meringues, 46
    Puffy Mallow Snowballs, 125
    Raspberry, 127
        Refrigerator, 127
    Shakes, Purple Cow, 18
    Soda, Strawberry, 20
    Sundae(s)
        Cereal, 21
        Hot Fudge, 146
        Jeweled, 21
        Steamboats, 22
Indian Maize Pancakes, 77
Italian
    Salads with Bambinos, 114
    Spaghetti, One-Pot, 89

J

Jelly
    -Coconut Frosting, 134
    Grape, Rosy, 49
Jeweled Sundaes, 21
Juicy Hamburgers, 88

L

Lace Frosting, 134
Lettuce-Tomato, Chicken-
        Bacon-, Salads, 117
Little
    Brown Hens, 150
    Pumpkin Cups, 37
Lollipops, 30
Luncheon Meat-Biscuit Bake,
    97

M

Macaroni
    Bologna Daisies and, 101
    Tuna Casserole, 104
Mallow Apples in the Coals,
    63
Marshmallow(s)
    Custards, 129
    Mallow Apples in the Coals,
        63
    Mallow Snowballs, Puffy, 125
    Puffs, 25
Mashed Potatoes, 120
Meat. See name of meat.
Meat loaf. See Beef, Meat Loaf.
Meatballs, Bumpy, 89
Menus
    Backward Dinner, 145–148
    Dad's Day Cookout,
        152–154
    Family Breakfast, 142–144
    Mom's Day Dinner, 149–151
Meringue(s)
    Pie
        Blue, 138
        Pink, 138
    Pink Elephant, 46
Merry-Go-Round Salad, 153
Mexican Cookies, 30
Milk
    Chocolate, 64
    Cocoa, 19
    Eggnog, Snowcap, 20
    Shakes, Purple Cow, 18
Milk Chocolate Brownie Cake,
    131
Muffins, Surprise, 79
Munchy Crunchy Granola, 20
Mustard seeds, growing, 118

N

No-Cook Cherry Divinity, 35
No-Crust Wide-Eyed Pizzas, 90
Noodle(s)
    Nests, 36
    Soup, Chicken, 55

O

One-Pot Italian Spaghetti, 89
Onion Rings, Baked Fish with, 106
Open-Face Hamburgers, 68
Orange
    Cream Shortcakes, 136
    Junior, Banana-, 19
    Shortcakes, Strawberry-, 136
    Sip, 62
    Tapioca, Creamy, 129
Oven Cobblestone Stew, 86

P

Pancake(s)
    Apple-Sausage, 75
    Banana, 74
    Dit Dit Dot, 74
    Indian Maize, 77
    Round-Up, 75
    Syrup, Homemade, 77
Peach Double Deckers, 135
Peanut(ty)
    Butter
        Crunchy, Homemade, 48
        Smooth, 48
    Chocolate Pie, 140
    Egg Salad-, Sandwiches, 67
    Pretzels, 80
Peppermint Taffy, 52
Pick-a-Fruit Platter, 144
Pick-Your-Flavor Cookies, 28
Pickles, Dillybobs, 58
Pie(s)
    Chocolate, Peanutty, 140
    Meringue
        Blue, 138
        Pink, 138
    Sherbet, in Coconut Crust, 140
Pineapple(s)
    Frankabobs, 58
    -Ham Haystacks, 69
    Pick-a-Fruit Platter, 144
Pink
    Elephant Meringues, 46
    Meringue Pie, 138

Pink (cont.)
    or Yellow Banana Yum-Yums, 16
Pinwheels, 30
Pizza(s)
    No-Crust Wide-Eyed, 90
    Polka Dot, 71
    Shrimpy, 69
Poached-Fried Egg, 103
Polka Dot Pizzas, 71
Popcorn Ring Centerpiece, 47
Pops
    Hawaiian, 18
    Pudding, 18
Porcupine Salads, 113
Pork. See also Bacon;
        Bologna; Frankfurters;
        Ham; Sausage.
    Chops, Yummy, 146
    Luncheon Meat-Biscuit Bake, 97
    Ribs, Sticky Barbecued, 100
    Tenderloins, Baked, 100
Potato(es)
    Baked, 148
    in Meat Loaf Rings, 94
    -Egg Scramble, 56
    Mashed, 120
    Potatobobs, 58
Pound Cake with Pokey
        Frosting, 132
Pretzels
    Cheesy, 80
    Frosted, 52
    Peanutty, 80
Pudding
    Double Deckers, 135
    Pops, 18
Puffy Mallow Snowballs, 125
Pumpkin
    Cups, Little, 37
    Loaf, Golden, 37
Purple Cow Shakes, 18

Q

Quick
    Date Cake, 130
    Orange-, 130

Quick (cont.)
    Chix on Stix, 60
    -Energy Pickups, 32
    Soup with Rice, 55

R

Radishes
    Raw Vegetable Snacks, 23
    Vegetable Bugs, 23
Raspberry
    Ice Cream, 127
        Refrigerator, 127
    Spin, 128
Raw Vegetable Snacks, 23
Red and White Trifle, 137
Refried Beans, Tacos Sealed
        with, 92
Rhubarberry Sauce, 124
Rice, Quick Soup with, 55
Rock Cornish hens, Little
        Brown Hens, 150
Rocky Road
    Frosting, 132
    Fudge, 49
Root Beer
    Cookies, 27
    Spin, 128
Rosy Grape Jelly, 49
Round-Up Pancakes, 75

S

Salad(s)
    Chicken-Bacon-Lettuce-Tomato, 117
    Coleslaw, Crunchy, 113
    Daisy, 148
    Firecracker, 112
    Friendly Dog, 110
    Fruits on Skewers, 111
    Ham Roll-Ups with
        Cantaloupe Wedges, 111
    in a Bag, 119
    Italian, with Bambinos, 114
    Merry-Go-Round, 153
    Porcupine, 113

Salad(s) *(cont.)*
    Volcano, 116
    Walking, 54
    Watermelon Star, 112
    Yellow-Haired Girl, 111
Sandwich(es)
    Cheese, Baked, 67
    Egg Salad, 67
      -Peanut, 67
    Hamburgers. *See* Beef,
      Hamburger(s).
    Hot dogs. *See* Frankfurters.
    Pineapple-Ham Haystacks,
      69
    Sloppy Joes, 88
    Steak, Double, 57
    Tuna
      Chunky, 66
      Hot, 66
Sausage
    Bratwurst, Bites, 143
    Pancakes
      Apple-, 75
      Dit Dit Dot, 74
Shake-Em-Up Scrambled Eggs,
    143
Shakes, Purple Cow, 18
Sherbet Pie in Coconut Crust,
    140
Shortcakes. *See* Cake(s),
    Shortcakes.
Shrimpy Pizzas, 69
Sizzling Hamburgers, 153
Sloppy Joes, 88
Smooth Peanut Butter, 48
S'More, 64
Snowcap Eggnog, 20
Soda
    Pop, Campers' Foaming, 64
    Strawberry, 20
Soup
    Bean, Best, 122
    Beef-Vegetable, 120
    Chicken Noodle, 55
    Quick, with Rice, 55
Spaghetti, One-Pot Italian, 89
Spareribs, Sticky Barbecued
    Ribs, 100
Spicy Date Softies, 29
Spreads
    Jelly, Rosy Grape, 49

Spreads *(cont.)*
    Peanut Butter
      Homemade Crunchy, 48
      Smooth, 48
Sprinkle Cookies, 24
Squash, Easy Baked, 122
Steak. *See* Beef, Steak(s).
Sticky Barbecued Ribs, 100
Strawberry(-ies)
    Firecracker Salads, 112
    -Orange Shortcakes, 136
    Rhubarberry Sauce, 124
    Soda, 20
    Squares, 32
Stretchy French Loaf, 84
String Frosting, 134
Sugar Babies, 62
Sundae(s). *See also* Ice Cream.
    Steamboats, 22
Surprise Muffins, 79
Syrup, Homemade Pancake, 77

T

Taco(s)
    Sealed with Refried Beans, 92
    -Taco Fish Sticks, 108
Taffy, Peppermint, 52
Tapioca, Creamy Orange, 129
Tart Shells, Fluted, 137
Teddy Bear Paws, 30
Texas-Style Chili, 57
Toast. *See* Bread(s).
Toasty Hot Dog Roll-Ups, 68
Tomato(es)
    -Bean Bake, Cheesy, 146
    Mush, 23
    Salad(s)
      Chicken-Bacon-Lettuce, 117
      in a Bag, 119
    Vegetable Bugs, 23
Trifle, Red and White, 137
Tuna
    Casserole, 104
    Chow Mein, 105
    Sandwiches
      Chunky, 66
      Hot, 66
Twin Eggs in Toast Basket, 103

V

Vegetable(s). *See also name of
    vegetable.*
    Bean(s)
      Bake, Cheesy Tomato-, 146
      Green, Crunchy, 151
    Beef-, Soup, 120
    Bugs, 23
    Carrot Sticks, Buttered, 121
    Corn
      Cheese-Scalloped, 121
      in the Coals, 61
      on the Cob, 121
    Potato(es)
      Baked, 148
      Mashed, 120
    Snacks, Raw, 23
    Squash, Easy Baked, 122
    Tomato-Bean Bake, Cheesy,
      146
Volcano Salads, 116

W

Waffles, 73
    Blueberry, 73
Walking Salads, 54
Watermelon Star Salad, 112
Wheaten Loaf, 82

Y

Yellow
    Banana Yum-Yums, Pink or,
      16
    -Haired Girl Salad, 111
Yo-Yo Cookies, 26
Yummy Pork Chops, 146

Z

Zingy Horseradish Meat Loaf, 93
Zucchini, Raw Vegetable
    Snacks, 23